DAMNATIO MEMORIAE

Sebastian Barker

Damnatio Memoriae

Erased from Memory

Only what word
Wisest my heart breeds dark heaven's baffling ban
Bars or hell's spell thwarts.

ENITHARMON PRESS

First published in 2004
by the Enitharmon Press
26B Caversham Road
London NW5 2DU

www.enitharmon.co.uk

Distributed in the UK by
Central Books
99 Wallis Road
London E9 5LN

Distributed in the USA and Canada
by Dufour Editions Inc.
PO Box 7, Chester Springs
PA 19425, USA

ISBN 1 900564 09 2

Enitharmon Press gratefully acknowledges the financial support of
Arts Council England, London.

British Library Cataloguing-in-Publication Data.
A catalogue record for this book is available
from the British Library.

Typeset in Bembo by Servis Filmsetting Ltd
and printed in England by
Antony Rowe Ltd

Dedicated to Daniel and Xanthi

ACKNOWLEDGEMENTS

Grateful acknowledgements are made to the editors of the following publications in which most of these poems first appeared. *Acumen, Blade, Iron, PNReview, Poetinis Druskininky/Druskininkai Poetic* (Vaga, Lithuania, 2003), *Poetry London, Poetry Scotland, Temenos Academy Review, The Interpreter's House, Chapman, Tuba, Scintilla, The Manchester Cathedral Religious Poetry Competition* (The Chapter of Manchester Cathedral), *The Road to Parnassus* (University of Salzburg), *The Sonnet at the Millennium* (The Open University Shakespeare Society), *The Times Literary Supplement / Poems on the Underground* (Cassell Publishers and The Times Literary Supplement). 'Curriculum Vitae' was commissioned by John Heath-Stubbs for the Omar Khayyám Society. 'The Teraphim of Trash' was the model for an eponymous monumental sculpture in Bath stone (2002) by Paul Bothwell Kincaid.

CONTENTS

1. Curriculum Vitae   9

Curriculum Vitae   11
The Ballad of Hackney Brook   13
Katie   15
I Hear the Wood Doves Cooing in the Trees   16
On My Daughter Returning After Long Absence   17
A Book   18
In the Heart of Hackney   19
Linger Awhile   20
Silent Meditation   21
Sparks From the Anvil   22

2. On The Anvil of the Tongue   25

The Open Plan   27
Sex   28
Marriage   29
Take hands. The moon   30
Sacred Image of the Face   31
The Venus Virgin   32
The Virgin Muse   33
Parmenides and the Venus Virgin   34
The Animated Dynamo   35
The Virgin Watchdog   36
Speculum Sine Macula   38
I Went to Work on the Way to School   40
I Caught the Glimpse of a Golden Ray   42
On the Anvil of the Tongue   44

The Visitors   45
Tell of the Sad Derangement of the Mind   47

3. The Uncut Stone   49

Father Alban   51
Peter Russell's Dream   52
On the Resurrection of Basil Hume   54
Athenagoras   55
Holy the Heart on which We Hang Our Hope   57
A Song for Sarah   58
In the Valley of the Moselle   60
The Rites Mysterious   61
The Artists of the Grape   62
The Uncut Stone   63

Notes to sections 1, 2 and 3   65

4. Damnatio Memoriae   67

Damnatio Memoriae: Erased from Memory   69
Columbarium: An Eclogue from the Auvergne   74
The Scribe in the Scriptorium   79
The Teraphim of Trash   84
The Argosy of Faith   89
Against the Deadening of the Mind   94

The Exegesis   99

CURRICULUM VITAE

Curriculum Vitae

Curriculum vitae? Still alive.
Born – in 1945.
Prep and public school. Imprudent
Imbiber, yet a zealous student.

Oxford science. Why we breathe
At all, let alone conceive.
Research proved boring. On the whole
Science procrastinates the soul,

Whose true anatomy is hurt
Into the beautiful by art.
East Anglia University
Conferred an English Lit degree.

Next, six bright years of scrubbing wood
To earn an honest livelihood.
A carpenter. A fireman. 'What the hell!'
We roared while clanging on the bell.

My first collection, cloth and printed
Like legal tender newly minted,
Looked on kitchen tables for
First love in 1974.

Disaster struck my proud young head.
Divorce, like marriage, starts in bed.
Trudging London, now a squatter,
Luck turned master of the matter.

A job in Sotheby's, no less,
Cataloguing dead success.
The boneyard of literature I knew
In all its breadth at 32.

Pressure-cooked by such vocation,
I tasted breakdown for a season,
But, resurrected by the art
Of fiction, made a flying start

Out of myself into the story
Of one worse off, yet nudging glory.
Eddie Linden is his name
Of Irish, gay, and Catholic fame.

A job in Berkshire. Then the air
Of Greece (blue skies throughout a year)
Building a house in which to make
A poem for my dead friends' sake;

And all who, death being sure predicted,
Find themselves a touch afflicted.
Seven years in that furnace, then
The poem like a horse was born

White hot, winged, and snorting fire.
In print, black ash, for sale or hire.
Now if you think this makes me sad,
There's one last snippet to be had.

The Poetry Society. I met one there,
The soul and party, the affair
Of my mid-age, who brings me peace,
Her love, where paranoias cease.

The Ballad of Hackney Brook

Gone is the blood of the tortured eye.
   Gone, gone is the strain.
Those who've suffered know what it's like
   To feel the end of pain.

Freedom shines on the Hackney streets,
   Freedom shines on the hills,
Freedom shines on the garden plots,
   The lust-proof daffodils.

In Clissold Park, it's a blazing day,
   Mothers go mothering by,
A man upright on a monobike,
   The steeple in the sky.

Wild birds chirrup in a bush,
   Plane trees dance with light,
Glad dogs race from place to place,
   Seagulls circulate.

On a bench in this park in my early years,
   When I lived on Highbury Hill,
I saw those squawkers circulate
   Circulating still.

Two willows hang on the Brook. The sun
   Cracks the safe of the cloud.
A young man walks as I once walked,
   Haunted, hallowed, proud.

Life comes down like a ton of bricks.
   Thirty years crash by.
The new look on the Hackney Brook
   Directs my flashing eye

To the dunking duck, the raucous goose,
   The swan's historic neck,
For next to love I know no love
   Like the love of Hackney Brook.

Katie

O Katie, my Katie,
　　There was none like you
Seated on your barstool
　　To drink the whole night through.

No man dared approach you
　　So dazzling were you then,
Blue hoops around your jumper,
　　White jeans around your groin.

You sat cross-legged and upright
　　With cigarette and wine,
Your head as hard as granite,
　　Your smile as soft as rain.

I loved you through two summers,
　　I'll love you when we're dead,
Hand in hand through Hyde Park
　　Fresh from my teenage bed.

O Katie, my Katie,
　　There was none like you
Seated on your barstool
　　Immaculate and true.

I Hear the Wood Doves Cooing in the Trees

I hear the wood doves cooing in the trees.
Softer music hurts me, for I hear
The sharp and clarion of my mother's voice
Imitate the wood doves to summon us to her.

Her presence warmed, like witnessing a smile
Come to the face of the long since haunted.
Nothing was too much for her, the pail
Of icy water clanking on the floor.

The kitchen was her coronet, her crown.
Her sandaled feet were purposeful and sure.
She took us in her arms, her dusty children,
At two, or six, or more than forty-four.

Some come born with sunlight. She was one.
And to her language light and love are gone.

On My Daughter Returning after Long Absence

for Chloë

Morning crackles with a thousand lives
In Kentish Town. A woodpecker taps a tree.
I note how the silence of a rose revives
My flagging mind with what it is to be.

The stillness of its adoration speaks
A tender prose so softly I can hear
How much it loves the sun because it makes
The distances between them disappear.

And so, my darling daughter, like a rose
I bathe in the sunshine of your presence now
Love without limit, which a father knows,

Beams from your being (your incandescence shows)
Light without limit to my blackest brow.
Pride in my daughter is what my eyes disclose.

A Book

for my daughter on her 21st birthday

Lean and learnèd language live
Nightly, brightly; set around her
Laughter, loyal, light, profounder
When the words are soaring; give

Her lodgings, candlelit, the look
Of students filleting a book
Lighting up the dark acreage
Of the mind, its psychopathic rage.

Beyond, the mountaintops of snow
Touching blue heaven, where people go
To understand themselves, their clobber
Aerodynamic, their God a

Parachutist from the sun
Explaining how such things are done.
This book the riddle in his hand, a
Birthday present for Miranda.

In the Heart of Hackney

for Aidan Andrew Dun

Behold, a swan. Ten houseboats on the Lee.
   A cyclist on the towpath. Gentle rain.
A pigeon in a white apple-blossom tree.
   And through the Marsh the rumble of a train.

Two courting geese waddle on the bank
   Croaking. A man unties his boat.
Police cars howl and whoop. And vast and blank
   The rain cloud of the sky is trampled underfoot.

Behold, a dove. And in Bomb Crater Pond
   Fat frogs ignore the rain.
Each trembling rush signals like a wand
   Earthing the magic of London once again.

In the heart of Hackney, five miles from Kentish Town,
By Lammas Lands the reed beds are glowing rich and brown.

Linger Awhile

Linger awhile. Tell me about the news.
Don't go just yet. I tinkered with the clock.
Pull up your chair again. Don't think it mean
To pinch an hour from me, your special friend.

Time snips the corners, whittling down
What little time we have to less than none.
Linger awhile. Tell me about your son
Who grew to be a master of the world.

Don't go. The berry leaves are green.
The milk is fresh. And on the Chinese screen
My life comes back to me, and with it, yours.
Don't go. The berry leaves are ours.

Hours and hours. The future has a price.
A jeroboam of wine ought to pay the bill.
The sun is tilting on the melting ice
And on the table top your hand is still.

Silent Meditation

A silence so perfect I can touch the air.
A fly might enter or a fly might leave.
This poem is an ecstasy, a despair,
Nor entranced by what it might believe.

Two roads to consider. One incessant flame
Burning in the fact we are alive
A moment too long because we learn the name
Of one more dearest friend gone to the grave.

Ecstatic reaction is a crime
Against the very delicacy we knew.
Despair perhaps the greater, the sublime
Holding its counsel, till the words ring true.

Two roads to consider. The second, play and player
The silent meditation of the prayer.

Sparks from the Anvil

YOUNG WOMAN DANCING

See, now, the yellow of her green, flamboyant dress
   Cavorting in the havoc of her legs' delight.
She does not care if she ignites distress
   Or the aurora borealis of my night.

SEXUAL LOVE

Soul of the butterfly
Undo me utterly.

WHEN ECSTASY COMES KNOCKING

When ecstasy comes knocking,
   Don't turn it from your door,
Don't turn away, politely mocking,
   As funless as before.

When ecstasy comes knocking,
   Open all the doors,
Open all the locks and windows,
   Let the bedroom blaze.

When ecstasy comes knocking,
   Knocking in your bones,
In your very windpipe knocking
   Your ecstasy to moans,

When ecstasy comes knocking,
   Don't turn it from your door,
Don't turn away, politely mocking,
   As funless as before.

A SMALL BALLET OF LIGHT

The tapping of a word processor
    In the summer garden
Mangles the morning
    To a pulp of literature.

The shadow of the lime tree
    Publishes the answer of the sun,
A small ballet of light
    On the table top.

THE BUDDHIST

A soul was clapping in the sole immense.
    Duty taught it, but the ease of soul
Was not in the audition, more the sense
    Of something far more mighty in control.

THE LILIES OF THE FIELD

Do not say the lilies of the field are wrong
Or what the inspired young say is the worthlessness of song.

Tenderness to the new is the mark of a wiser mind.
Infancy, like art, teaches us how to be kind.

THE PROOF

Do not come with the proof, which you are thinking of.
The inmost ground of the heart burns in the fury of love.

ON THE ANVIL OF THE TONGUE

The Open Plan

Drunken as a despot,
   Delinquent as a thief,
I trod the road to bitterness,
   The bitterness of grief.

Grief had gone bananas.
   I went that very way.
And though I lived to see it,
   I tremble to this day.

Grief had gone bananas.
   The pilots in the skies
Wept to put out
   The fire in their eyes.

Grief had gone bananas.
   Grief was tragedy,
Tragedy to hear,
   Tragedy to see.

So when I behold her
   On the Open Plan
Caress my very temperature
   Marriage has begun.

Sex

Speak of the time
    when sex has come
To a boy and a girl alive:
    in a bright shining lake
In a secret wood
    in a darkness deep as the grove.

Speak of the checks
    to limit the sex
Of the boy and the girl to this:
    in a grown-up bed
Words are said
    night after night after bliss.

Speak of the day
    when the nights are too
Short for the sum of the parts:
    working alone
Living as one
    in the glorious sex of their hearts.

Speak of the curse
    their actions arouse
In the waters of paradise lost:
    see how they swim
In the cock and the quim
    not waving not drowning but blest.

Speak of the acts
    their charter of sex
Hangs in the halls of the lands:
    the bright shining words
(Sheltered by God's)
    written by quivering hands.

Marriage

As blue as pity,
  With an Angel's face,
My muse destroys me
  With a lover's ease.

Backwards to the future,
  Backwards to the past,
She holds me in the present
  As long as presents last.

The going scares. The temperature
  Just went up today.
My muse is insatiable
  To display.

Solid soul, O sages,
  Regal in a gown,
Naked as a miracle,
  Soft as eiderdown.

As blue as pity,
  With an Angel's face,
My muse destroys me
  With a lover's ease.

Take hands. The moon

Take hands. The moon
Is rising on the barn.
The lime tree sheds its seeds.
The night is warm.

Take hands. Too soon
The lightning in your eyes
Like lightning in the skies
Succeeds

In lighting up the dawn
When both of us are gone.

Take hands. The moon
Has trebled now in size.
Our firm distinctions of its outline make
Our grip on logic shake.

Take hands. The night
Vanishes from sight.

Sacred Image of the Face

Sacred image of the face
   Yet grows on human jaws
Speaks of the commands of grace
   And yet gives human laws.

Tells of how the world began
   Tells of all the news
Breaking on the mind of man
   The Nazis and the Jews.

Tells of how the rockets came
   And blew our world apart
Tells of how the sacred name
   Stayed sacred in our art.

Tells of all that art's about
   The moral and the theme
O sacred image inside out
   Reality made dream.

The Venus Virgin

Her hips are wanton. I am not myself.
It does not seem unreasonable to me
I can not contain her hips, they are so wanton
I am deranged by what my eyes can see.

Glory of access is John Donne in tone.
That is not my pleasure nor my plea.
I want the singing rapture of the zone
Where all her love is evident to me.

Or you. Or men. Crossing the sea at night,
There must be those who want her, as I sing
The happy hips of rapture steer us right
Through the very ecstasy they bring.

She is our source of light. Let language sample
The Venus Virgin, who is our first example.

The Virgin Muse

Look on her once and know, the kneeling knee
Proud to submit to the known to be holy,
Toned in the azure of a loving mind
Commanding respect, respect of humankind.

Look on her once and speak, the encountering tongue
Reacting in a language no English poet has sung.
Look on her once and speak. The Virgin Muse.
To few souls ever popular. Whom none abuse.

The tabletop is teak. Sunlight slants the room
To a low-roofed triangle of pre-Euclidean light.
The murmur of the wood doves consecrates the gloom.
The wind disrupts the trees. Down comes the night.

Look on her once and know, the kneeling knee
Proud to submit to the known to be holy.

Parmenides and the Venus Virgin

Sphinx to reason, sacred as the day
When the great Parmenides sat down to write,
I see the wheels of what I have to say
Break on the beauty which you command tonight.

Two ways there are, so the great man taught,
To live on earth. One is to inquire
To know the truth. The other to be bought,
Bullied, bound, and butchered by desire.

He did not teach desire on its own
Misled, but desire coupled to opinion.
Desire to inquire to know the truth was known
By his pupil Plato to reach the true union.

The Greeks were right. Desire to look on you
Was never more necessary, never more true.

The Animated Dynamo

Neither Diana of the Ephesians nor any of the Oriental
goddesses was worshipped for her beauty. She was
goddess because of her force; she was the animated dynamo.
Henry Adams, *The Education of Henry Adams*

Split by the dynamo is the holy cross
The holy heart of woman and the cast-iron boss

The dynamo is dynamite dancing on the wheels
When all the world is functioning some know how it feels

Whirling like a hurricane generating rain
Illuminating Chartres Cathedral in its iron brain

The dynamo is dynamite wedded to its breast
The holy heart of woman knows the dynamo is best

The dynamo is dynamite ecstasy on wheels
The cross and the boss and the atom as it reels

The Virgin Watchdog

Another middle-age departure
Of Apollo from the trade of archer.
Grab your hat and coat, my girl,
We're going on a conscious whirl,
Out the mouths of bar-room hacks,
Out of lovers' bending backs,
Out of sight and out of mind,
Travellers to a far-off land.

Touch of foot and down we are
In concrete arches wide and far.
Spaghetti junction drips with rain,
A circuit in Apollo's brain.
The beggar lying in the street
Accepts Apollo's golden foot.
The merciless, the culprits feel,
The Dionysian heel.

On we go. The city park
Sees people ambling as they talk,
Each unafraid and sober eye
Acknowledging each passer-by.
The lake like mercury distills
Sunny clouds from greasy tills;
The city just, the culprit's lair,
Guarded by Athena's spear.

On we go. The conscious flames
In marble and in cardboard homes
Ignite the torch of Aphrodite,
Naked nude, the scorching beauty.
The Virgin Watchdog reaches down
And clothes her in a buckled gown,
Forged from iron, spun from stone,
Tripartite in the Three-in-One.

Speculum Sine Macula

Speak, O Mirror, on the wall,
Who is the fairest of them all?
Virgin Mother? Venus? Child?
Father mad? Or Father mild?
Speak, O Mirror, on the wall,
Who is the fairest of them all?

Speak, O Mirror, cold as ice,
Tell me who the fairest is.
Is it Mother? Is it Child?
Is it Venus? Weak or wild?
Speak, O Mirror, cold as ice,
Is it Father first in place?

Speak, O Mirror, hot as fire,
Tell me who the fairest are.
All are fair, no doubt, but stain
Attaches to no fairest one.
Speak, O Mirror, hot as fire,
Tell me what I most desire.

Speak, O Mirror, wise as Christ,
Tell me who the fairest is.
'The fairest of the fair is who
The others lift their eyes up to.'
Speak, O Mirror, wise as Christ.
'Their eyes up to the one who is.'

Speak, O Mirror, teach me words
Fairer than the one that plods.
'Fair is God and fair is she
Who holds to God's priority.
Fair is she who Jesus bore,
Fair is she who beauty wore.'
Speak, O Mirror, teach me words.
'The fairest of them all are God's.'

I Went to Work on the Way to School

I went to work on the way to school.
I went to work on the way things are.
I re-defined the metre rule
The metre of the avatar.
I stole from college books the full
Catastrophe, the fallen star.
Men, women, children, the saint or fool,
I went to work on the way to school.

I went to work on the way to bed.
I went to work on a pinch of corn.
I re-arranged the holy head
The image of our being born.
I stole from college books the red
Hot words no scholars scorn.
And as I worked my image bled.
I went to work on the way to bed.

I went to work on the way to sleep.
I went to work on the image hard.
I re-deployed the image deep
In English turf, the Sleeping Lord.
I stole from college books the keep
And conduct of the word.
And as I worked I woke to weep.
I went to work on the way to sleep.

I went to work on the way to die.
I went to work on the way things are.
I re-examined ear and eye
Conscious of the fallen star.
I stole from college books the high
Logic of the holy law.
And as I worked I torched the sky.
I went to work on the way to die.

I went to work on the way to live.
I went to work on the way things are.
I re-created man alive
In paint and poem, schooled and raw.
I stole from college books the give
And take I take no more.
And as I work I work with love.
I went to work on the way to live.

I Caught the Glimpse of a Golden Ray

I caught the glimpse of a golden ray
Some years ago. Those years have gone.
But as I heard, that melody,
That golden ray, is far from done.
And as I walk through the summer day,
Through forests, or through Merlin's tomb,
Or through the eye of a needle, say,
I caught the glimpse of a golden ray.

I caught the glimpse of a golden song
That very day. And on that day
A chance encounter happened along.
A woman said she knew the way
To peace, to home. Nor was she wrong.
At home – I sat. Or should I say
I lay with her all winter long.
I caught the glimpse of a golden song.

I caught the glimpse of a golden life
In London and in half of France.
The work was hard, the going rough,
Nor emptied of its elegance.
Times will change and change is tough.
We experienced the horror of the dance.
We experienced the trouble and the strife.
I caught the glimpse of a golden life.

I caught the glimpse of a golden work
Those years around. And as I age
Distance brings the present back.
I open out the golden page,
I read aloud the golden book.
And there the evil rant and rage,
And there the evil go berserk.
I caught the glimpse of a golden work.

On the Anvil of the Tongue

Terror conscience struck me down.
  The bad old days had come,
Conscience sunken, fit to drown,
  An anvil round its tongue.

Terror conscience struck me hard.
  The beatings had begun,
Beatings fit to break the word
  On the anvil of the tongue.

Terror conscience took my sex,
  Sprayed it with a gun,
Sprayed it fit to break yours next
  On the anvil of the tongue.

Terror conscience knows no bounds,
  No circle to its aims.
The heads of state, the diamond hoards,
  Attract its wicked ends.

Terror conscience guards the words
  To offset these laws
Crouched at home with fourteen leopards
  In its iron claws.

The Visitors

When they come, they come with accusing eyes.
  Their habits now are formed.
Who are they? No particulars
  Are visible or named.

When they come, they tap on your private door.
  There's nothing but – to do
What they tell you, when their eyes run cold
  And through you.

When they come, they do not come alone.
  They come with those to spare
All jocular and armed. They grin.
  You're bundled in a car.

When they come, they come on good advice.
  No cock-up, no misname.
They take you to a special place.
  They join you in the room.

When they come, they prod you on the chest.
  Questions cut like steel.
Seems you have a checkered past?
  Did you help at all?

When they come, they spin you round, a top
  Too terrified to move,
Too terrified, what's more, to stop.
  They have a point to prove.

They prove it with the single shot
    Flashing through your eyes.
They prove it with the frozen waste
    Where your carcass lies.

When they come, they come with accusing eyes.
    Their habits now are formed.
Who are they? No particulars
    Are visible or named.

Tell of the Sad Derangement of the Mind

for Harold Pinter

Tell of the sad derangement of the mind.
The wheat is being harvested. The sun
Shines on the bales, unclouded, unconfined.
Work as brisk as hard is being done.
Cider's drunk at night. Documents are signed.
The bedrooms warm. No licences on fun.
Tell of the sad derangement of the mind.
Tell of the sorrow nations cannot mend.

Tell of the sad derangement of the heart.
The wind is up and musical. The sky
Rolls over meadows, over cities, over cart
And Cadillac, the sanctum and the sty.
The blossom in the garden is not a thing apart.
Dinner's in the oven. Friends are dropping by.
Tell of the sad derangement of the heart.
Tell of the sorrow when nations have to part.

Tell of the sad derangement of the soul.
The wine is on the table. The talk is fine.
There's lamplight in the corner, the glowing coal,
Laughter from the kitchen, washing on the line.
Gourmets (fit to twist a knowing nostril) stroll
The happy halls. There's music. Pass the wine.
Tell of the sad derangement of the soul.
Tell of the sorrow when nations lose control.

Tell of the sad derangement of the man.
Sleep is in the doorway, and the night
Closes behind it. The fondest lovers yawn,
Fold themselves in beds both neighbourly and right.
A sanctuary of starlight protects them as they scan
The inner world of dreams, before the morning light.
Tell of the sad derangement of the man.
Tell of the sorrow before the world began.

THE UNCUT STONE

Father Alban

No fairer Father has a living man
   than he who makes it to a stranger's door
To find a fierce Franciscan beaming smiles
   fit to lift God knows how many
Centuries of grief. I walked beneath
   conscious of that strange phenomenon
The weightlessness of being. We wandered on
   down corridors and stairs
To what encounter in his tiny cell
   crammed with books and courtesy so sharp
We cut a friendship on the common air?
   And did we meet as I remember it?
'You have made me a happy man.'
   'Then you have made me a happier man,' he said.

Spinning with delight, my gyroscope of brain
   tried every angle in its new career.
All were steady. None could over-rock
   my patient progress down the River Thames
Along the long Embankment to a shop
   To buy a book his knowledge of my state
Knew how to name. In steep initiation
   I opened it at home and there I saw the
Catechism of the Catholic Church
   tunnelling time, edited by those
Who'd scrubbed that subway clean and studded it
   with jewelled mosaics. I took the book to bits
And found it made of human flesh and blood
   in which no fairer Father found his feet.

Peter Russell's Dream

Heavenly Mother, muse of my own heart,
   gather the imperium of bliss
Into your fist. Thump the scapular of cloud
   misinhabiting the sky.
Fumigate it, Ma'am. Scrub it clean,
   an open window on the wider world.
Peter walks the earth. Why not let him
   look up and see your understanding hand
Scoop him up and constitute him new,
   the old broke scholar-poet that he is,
Blazing praise through black-rimmed spectacles
   only the antique are young enough to sing?

Speak, Theotokos, roll a word
   into the whorled auditorium of his ear,
A pearl, Mother of Pearl,
   like a depth-charge sinking
Into the cold ocean of his blood.
   He will know
What you are doing. Blast the bleak
   deep with trinitrotoluene
Illumination, Duck. Let him see
   interior luminescence
In the heart of his own being
   light the world.

Plunder the dumb, steal the noise
    each cannot articulate.
Plunder the dud diocese of their brains
    peopling the earth.
Rip off their sound. Let them speak through him,
    'Mother of mercy, tentacle of belief,
Be more than the loud hosanna of our prayer.
    Teach us truth. Expel the explanation
Of cold-blooded murder before our eyes.
    Associate with hope.
And let the love you linger in remain.'
    Peter walks the earth

In Italy. His yellow beard compels
    the molecules of oxygen he breathes
To somersault his nicotined trachea
    crazy with the ecstasy you teach
In every mausoleum with your name.
    Mary marry mirth
With music. Make, shake, awake them, as they curl
    round Peter's pence like adamantine thread.
Trap the noble gold, the dust of gulls,
    who circulate the supersloop you sail;
For Peter dreams the dreadful dream of death,
    drowning anastatic in your arms.

On the Resurrection of Basil Hume

Tender person, witty man,
   how goes it now your pilgrimage is done,
The long, slow exodus from time?
   Do you rest in breathless
Silences of sound, no man made,
   nor exquisite composer,
Thomas-Tallis-like, instructs,
   but Christ himself conducts,
His batoned hand invisible to the eye
   of any but the infantine intelligence
Supertopping knowledge? What questions hook
   your shepherd's crook
Now all are answered?

Soul of reason incarnate in the faith
   your fellow bishops hold through bold catastrophe,
Reach up, not down, now all your work is done.
   Catch the cup the quiet barman chucks
Post Christ in concert. Sip the liquor neat.
   Lean on the bar of burnished Burmese teak
To cull the conversation of the crowd.
   Tease out the tumbling talk, the terror-red
Reverence, the white-hot words they speak:
   'We were expecting you.
Turn and see the only explanation
   within the mirrored bar of why you are,
The Holy Father blazing in your being.'

Athenagoras

Deep in the midnight of my Christmas heart,
    Athenagoras came, a whole world apart.
He taught me what the reindeer know,
    who sniff the interglacial snow.
He taught me what the termites feel
    incessant in their hopeful hill.
He taught me what the rivers say,
    which slice through continents of clay.
Like phosphorescent fish that burn,
    he taught me what the martyrs learn.
We know the truth. We know the lie.
    We do not live until we cannot die.

The megabucks, the superstars,
    the mobile phones in mobile cars,
The perky poet, the lucid don,
    the Valley of the Silicon,
Lace our language, chip the head,
    eclipse the unremembered dead.
The junk hawk drills his thinning skin
    to pump the lethal liquid in.
Like children surfing on the net,
    he taught me what the wise forget.
We know the truth. We know the lie.
    We do not live until we cannot die.

Get up, my darling, shake the sheets.
　　No blissy-wipe-out bed competes.
The ruddy rocks are red with blood
　　insurgent in our saviour's head.
What made us makes us what we are
　　when he becomes the evening star
And like the planet rolls away
　　the giant circumference of day
And leaves us in his rocklike hands
　　Athenagoras understands.
We know the truth. We know the lie.
　　We do not live until we cannot die.

Holy the Heart on which We Hang Our Hope

Holy the heart on which we hang our hope.
To trust in Christ is to trust him in the torture.
Shall we believe in pastor, priest, or pope?

The love of God is learning how to cope.
I don't believe in the God you don't believe in either.
Holy the heart on which we hang our hope.

Love is a ditch in which the shallow drown.
To trust in Christ is to trust him in the torture.
Sweet is the carriage in which we come to town.

The mind like a drunkard staggers on alone.
I don't believe in the God you don't believe in either.
The sink of Sheol opens in the bone.

Love is a ditch in which the shallow drown.
The love of God is learning how to cope.
Sweet is the carriage in which we come to town.
Holy the heart on which we hang our hope.

A Song for Sarah

Out of the whirlwind
   Poetry comes
Voicing the flutes
   Of a million drums.

Blood in my arteries
   Races like light
Shooting through heavens
   Of infinite night.

    Sarah Gray, Sarah Gray,
      I think of you, Sarah,
    And I'm blown away.

Sensations of seeing you
   Living on earth
Surpass all the estimates
   Money is worth.

Down on my knees
   In a city of steel
I know how the luckiest
   Billionaires feel.

    Sarah Gray, Sarah Gray,
      I think of you, Sarah,
    And I'm blown away.

Boiling like bitumen
   Holy as nuns
The forces between us grow
   Hotter than suns.

Love of my neighbour
   For that's who you are
Generates energy
   Stronger than war.

     Sarah Gray, Sarah Gray,
      I think of you, Sarah,
     And I'm blown away.

Out of the furnace
   Of making, erupt,
O superbright luminous
   Angel of love.

In the whirlwind of poetry
   More ecstasy than chaste
We are the man and woman
   The Angel has graced.

     Sarah Gray, Sarah Gray,
      I think of you, Sarah,
     And I'm blown away.

In the Valley of the Moselle

I love you, yes, with all my heart
   Pounding on my hotel bed,
Shafts of sunlight streaming through
   The strictest studies in my head.
Curves of concupiscence keep
   None so comely as your own:
My heart is pounding on my bed,
   My arms around you – cut in stone –

Behold the river running by
   The hotel window, where we drink
Shafts of sunlight in the wine
   As subtle as the thoughts we think.
I love you, yes, with all my mind
   Racing round the summer air,
Down the river valley, up
   Ecstatic vineyards everywhere.

I love you, yes, with all my soul
   Breaking through the light of dawn
Shattering the sheets of night
   In which the darkest souls are born.
I love you, yes, with all my strength
   Waking in the old hotel.
O hold, O holy heart, O hold
   My hand, entranced by the Moselle.

The Rites Mysterious

Holy spirit, let me be
The vessel of your poetry.

Open your door and let me in
The noble rapture of your skin.

Discard your jewels, let your rose
Be the meaning they disclose.

Take me to your kitchen, where
That banquet of your bed's laid bare.

Feast on the fortune of our lives
Where sacrament's sensation thrives.

Enrich the nakedness of heaven
As surely as a soul forgiven.

Impassioned by the word alone
Bind me to your very own.

Bound on the altar of one heart
Let us in ecstasy depart.

The Artists of the Grape

Slowly, slowly, rings the bell,
   Focus on the steeple, where
   The artists of the grape prepare,
Husbanding the sweet Moselle.

In chains of generation feel
   The steep-sloped care-combed vineyards praise
   Electric sunlight, rainy days,
Outlasting Rome or German steel.

Gently, gently, rings the bell,
   The artists of the grape prepare
   To suffer grace, none more aware
Than those who harrow the Moselle.

In chains of generation, they,
   The wooden vat, the trellised grape,
   Quit the unbecoming hope,
Become the artist's artistry.

Slowly, slowly, rings the bell,
   Focus on the steeple, where
   The artists of the grape prepare,
Husbanding the sweet Moselle.

The Uncut Stone

'a stone was cut out, not by human hands' (*Daniel* 2:34)
'the cornerstone cut out without hands' (Justin Martyr, *Dialogue with Trypho*)

Sunsets blazing out of my head,
   Burnt-out midnights moving on,
Nothing remains of the life I led,
   Clean as the wind-swept sky, I'm gone.
Nobody loses, nobody gains
   A drop of water in a thousand springs.
Not a trace of my life, not a trace remains.
   I am the voice of the ancient things.
   I am the audience nobody sings.

I come from the valley of the uncut stone,
   A spark from the furnace in my father's eye.
I belong with the muscles of the dancing bone
   In the womb of my mother in her ecstasy.
Nobody noticed, nobody saw
   What being (a babe in the wilderness) brings:
The more I advance, the more I withdraw.
   I am the voice of the ancient things.
   I am the audience nobody sings.

In my years of cutting the linguists' key
   To the door of the dungeon of the dispossessed,
I descended to the Pontiff of the Holy See
   Kneeling in the belly of the human beast.
What am I saying? Give me some air!
   Death is the death of a thousand stings.
The bloodier mortality, the bloodier the care.
   I am the voice of the ancient things.
   I am the audience nobody sings.

In the time of harvest our dust allows,
    I walk in the court of the uncut stone
Formed in the market, shadowed by trees,
    Circled by water, the sun and the moon.
Nobody prosecutes, chairs, or defends
    The court of the stone of the uncut wings
Of the whole of the harvest nobody ends.
    I am the voice of the ancient things.
    I am the audience nobody sings.

Notes to sections 1, 2 and 3

(pages 9–64)

(1) Title page epigraph, from 'To seem the stranger lies my lot, my life' by Gerard Manley Hopkins.

(2) 'Curriculum Vitae'. *The poem like a horse was born.* The reference is to a theory of art in Ancient Greece, in which the winged Pegasus, the work of art, is born from the throat of the decapitated Medusa.

(3) 'The Open Plan'. *The pilots in the skies / Wept to put out / The fire in their eyes.* A leading example of such a pilot is Leonard Cheshire (1917–92), bomber pilot, awarded the Victoria Cross in 1944. He was an official British observer of the destruction caused by the atomic bomb dropped on Nagasaki in 1945. *Tragedy to hear, / Tragedy to see.* There are circumstances in which the irreconcilable nature of memory is such that the act of hearing and the act of seeing cannot be distinguished from the perception of tragedy itself. *So when I behold her / On the Open Plan.* The Open Plan is the level of being on which the primordial and genuine truth of woman, experienced as pure beholding, dissolves the memory of the past to permit the appearance of the present and the future. Put another way, the oceanic quality of God finds in woman the receptacle in which to dissolve the pollution of a man's soul. *Caress my very temperature.* When the condition of a man's soul has become as hot as hell. The sexes in the poem may be reversed or made the same.

(4) 'The Virgin Watchdog'. *Another middle-age departure / Of Apollo from the trade of archer.* Patrick Kavanagh, 'Prelude'. The life of the humdrum man is transformed into that of the poet.

(5) 'Speculum Sine Macula'. Latin for the Spotless Mirror, an ancient title of the Blessed Virgin Mary.

(6) 'Athenagoras'. Athenagoras was a late 2nd century AD Greek philosopher known to Marcus Aurelius and his son Commodus. A treatise *On the Resurrection of the Dead* is traditionally ascribed to him. It is one of the most sophisticated treatments of the subject in the Christian canon. However, the attribution has been challenged. The poem is addressed to the author of the treatise, here called Athenagoras, whatever his actual name. *junk hawk*: heroin addict.

(7) 'A Song for Sarah'. Sarah Gray: a 21-year-old Essex girl working in an office in Piccadilly with my daughter Miranda.

(8) 'The Rites Mysterious'. *the rites / Mysterious of connubial love*, John Milton, *Paradise Lost*, bk. 4, 732–3.

(9) 'The Uncut Stone'. The uncut stone has an oriental counterpart in the uncarved block of the *Tao Te Ching*. That work is traditionally ascribed to Lao Tzu, an older contemporary of Confucius, who lived 551–479 BC. Modern scholars favour a source in the late 4th to early 3rd century BC.

DAMNATIO MEMORIAE

Erased from Memory

A Poem in Six Movements
Scored for Many Voices

Don't open the furnace door if you don't know how to close it.

With an Exegesis

Damnatio Memoriae

I

The arrows of the Almighty are in me;
  my spirit drinks their poison;
The terrors of God are pitched against me.
  Truly, God is a God
Who hides himself
  in the wadi of the willows
Under every green tree
  lost in loss itself.
As deep as Sheol, as high as heaven,
  I have searched for you, O God,
And found nothing. Yet I will praise you
  from the depths of my being
Eulogizing the abyss of divine charity,
  moaning with breaking heart and bitter grief.

II

I believe the notion of God essential to the mind.
  I believe divine power lifts a hand
Working visible things invisibly.
  Who dares calumniate the duty of holy love?
Love draws us closer than knowledge.
  I see its force, which cannot be made
But makes. I see its force, which causes
  wine to gladden the heart.
We are the wedding guests made beautiful
  by the indwelling of God in our reason.
But our ignorance of ourselves necessitates
  his incomprehensibility.
The wine-halls crumble; their builders lie
  bereft of bliss. Alas, bright cup!

III

I watch my friends, whose eyes are piercing,
  whose foreheads speak thought.
They know the experience of God
  indents the mind like a hallmark.
Does it remind them of the homeland of wanderers
  and the end of exile?
They say it is better for the scandal of God
  to erupt
Than the truth of it to be suppressed.
  The consecrated senses of the holy ones
Know empires collapse; the truth of God endures.
  Who will unlock the mystery of God?
Their speech is like a burning fire
  penetrating the secrets of my heart.

IV

Take this pain from me, I cry, for I cannot bear it.
  Your prayers are burning me.
The life of the solitary is the glory in the desert.
  Monks are the sinews of the church.
But money is the sinews of war;
  and the world is all that is the case,
Augustine's greatest miracle.
  But it, too, will be shaken
By sorrow and anguish,
  like a cloth shaken in the wind.
I read the history of Europe, the lectio divina,
  like the living devil rewriting the book of God.
A cockle-fish will cram the ocean into its shell
  sooner than the conceited will understand the divine.

V

Steeped in the depravity of conceit
   the language of men
Cannot comprehend
   heaven or hell.
The world is lit by the sunlight of the word,
   the holy word,
But the word moulders in dust and mildew.
   Men are the temple of the living God,
Said Paul. And of the living devil, we add.
   For churches never made anyone holy,
But men make churches holy,
   cities hell. What could be more simple?
The glory of God is a living man;
   and the life of man is the vision of God.

VI

I feel the touch of a saint's intelligence,
   a drop of water melting into sponge.
What bestial nature is as ferocious
   as human nature? he asks.
His sanctity shows itself, shorn of its rays,
   in the black fog of the Black Forest:
The Basque beggar saint
   with a furnace under his arm.
The unshakeable champion of true belief
   dictates to me. And as I write,
I wipe away my tears;
   tears roll down my face;
And though I steel my courage,
   I cannot hide the pain I feel.

VII

The discipline of silence is the nurse of speech.
    Reason compels the understanding to see.
The sons of wisdom are the church of the just,
    but the madness of the godless is more bitter than death.
The mind, like a drunkard, cannot find its home.
    The flesh is a wind that passes;
It does not come again.
    We are water spilled on the ground
Which cannot be gathered up.
    Shall we forget our misery
Like water that has passed away?
    Reason compels the understanding to see.
Wine is bottled poetry. Wheat is holy speech.
    The bread of charity is holy bread.

VIII

Generosity returns to its source.
    Reason in man is like God in the world.
No man has joy unless he lives in love;
    and we cannot love and not pity.
No one who loves Christ lost him in the torture.
    For God is the mind's true wealth;
He makes us rich
    in a superabundance
Beyond all question,
    the príma philosophía.
Philosophers are the lovers of God
    because God is another word for wisdom.
Aristotle called the study of truth
    philosophía or the love of wisdom.

IX

That is why Maimonides said,
   'The thorough understanding of Aristotle
Is the highest achievement to which man
   can attain, with the sole exception
Of the understanding of the prophets.'
   Do the philosophers and the prophets,
In the torrential flow of their eloquence,
   annul the full misery of our degradation?
And what is the truth about holiness?
   Is it that the more holy
A man is, the more his prayers plumb
   the bottomless convulsions of his weeping?
From all unbegun eternity, I see
   the indestructible rock of Christ abducting me.

X

Holy are those whom nature has not formed.
   Blest is the man whose woman comes from God.
God speaks the word and the word is clothed in flesh
   like a candle flame is cupped in wax.
Who will unlock the mystery of God?
   Each of us is to God
As the air to the sun that lights it.
   The poltroons, the popeholy, and the proud
Are like those who carry dust in the wind.
   The consecrated senses of the holy ones,
Those who close their eyes that they may see,
   know the land of the living, to which they go,
Is cut off by a deep divide
   from the land of the dying, in which we live.

Columbarium: An Eclogue from the Auvergne

I

Superliterate Mercurius Duplex boasts,
   I am the lowest of the low prima materia,
And the highest of the high lapis philosophorum.
   They call me Mercurius utriusque capax,
Mercury capable of both. I am
   the giant of twofold substance,
The symbol of the spirit. I am
   the Holy Spirit, the summum bonum,
And the Evil One, the summum malum.
   The paterfamilias of our ecclesia
Closes the codex and leads us to the cloisters.
   For we are the monks of prayer, the oratores,
Walking the honey-scented air
   in our monastery of light.

II

The mountains weave a patchwork quilt of yellow and green.
   The grey skies are flecked with low-flying crows.
We're talking fame barometers, financial hammocks,
   crushing oblivion, and minds that have lost
Philosophical sensitivity. Doing good science, we argue,
   does not justify – doing philosophy badly.
When the great gift of vision is gone,
   why does the God-denying fool insist
On the absolute trivialization of reality?
   Throughout the idiom of the night, dawn advances.
Light falls on our beds like an ascetic lover.
   We are reminded of a long-forgotten experience
Of so deep a core of union
   as to defy description.

III

In the exhilarating chill of a summer dawn,
   a sprocket of bright white moon
Hangs in the dark blue sky.
   As we gather our wits under the stone nave,
Music recreates the waterfall of faith.
   We shoot it once again in the Eucharist:
Our minds are at home
   in the spacious circuits of our reasoning.
For we have heard the raw music of the marketplace.
   We have served the husband and the wife
Co-equal in care. But we have been injected
   with the juices of ecstasy,
Like the rainbow
   endlessly inventing itself.

IV

This is the poem the raptorial eye
   writes to unite truth and pleasure;
A case of imagination
   attaching wings to stone.
For ours is the music of the great cathedrals,
   the emporia of praise.
These are the letters fixing the flux
   of our experience crossing
A bridge over Eden.
   Even as our abbot closes the scriptorium,
We gaze on the omphalos in the cloisters,
   a fountain of river water splashing in the sunlight.
For we are the scholastici whose brains are frying
   on the gridirons of the Mercurius.

V

'The great thing is not to be overtaken by envy.'
   'For what is more wretched than envy?'
'God is not a person, except in Christ.'
   And so we talk. Or quote, 'I continue my course
With the precision and security of a sleepwalker.'
   An alchemystical philosopher retorts,
'A vision is a dream breaking through
   the waking state of consciousness.'
'And the jewel of Heraclitus,' says another,
   'is that he saw the fundamental stuff
Has intelligence, is intelligence, is *the* intelligence.'
   A small river with the gift of grace
Rolls through the nightly walls out to the starry forest,
   the moon sharp as an icicle.

VI

The internal mechanism of the poem?
   The lovely insouciance of a friend?
What does the soul-branching of a tree
   teach us in the long, warm afternoons,
When the sad ghost of Coleridge beckons from the shadows?
   The leaves weigh the light
In the microbalance of their stillness.
   In the dark directory of ear and eye,
A few poor words are registered.
   'In search of God, I made my way
Through the enormity of day.'
   Later, by a glass of wine on a wooden table
Serene as a ruby, like a lake contained,
   'That I understand, I do not understand.'

VII

What is the secret music of the intellect?
   What is the practical virtue of the same?
The innocence of the artist is a paradise of intuition
   at work in the darkness of an ageless agony.
The chestnut and the tulip give
   no sense of an alternative.
They know enough who know how to learn.
   In the preconceptual life of the intellect,
We bathe in the river as naked as a prayer.
   A wild rose plucked in a storm
Is not more amazing
   than the place on which we're gazing.
It is the zonulet of love,
   the bubbling of water around a sunken stone.

VIII

Like disembodied minds wandering the cut stone
   colder than a Gallic winter;
Half-drowned in Burgundian wine;
   or shelling peas in a silver dish at dusk;
We reassemble our nerves in a trough of snow-cooled water,
   a donkey of Corinthian bronze
Hard by us on the terracotta sideboard,
   its panniers bulging with fresh black olives.
A well-provoked gridiron steaming with sausages
   restores us to sense, though one of us complains,
'I scurry about like a mouse in a chamber pot.'
   Yet his soul is in his nose, I can tell you,
Ready to be blown. He steps straight out, like a new man,
   an incredible tumult of idea and significance.

IX

The sound of kissing, endlessly beginning,
    barges chortling down the Rhône, endlessly.
'Dip your head, my dolly swan,
    feast in what you're floating on.'
Aeroplanes poised like mosquitoes
    take off in a sun like the imagination:
Harmless until it sets the woods on fire.
    The grey owl of poetry glides through
The penetralium of the word.
    We inhale the oxygen of praise,
Then rubberstamp the innocent to confirm
    nature's cruel holiness.
The birds in the trees
    forgive our eccentricities.

X

There is more of the miraculous
    in the clouds of milk entering a cup of tea
Than in the minds of the irreverent.
    We sip our honey-golden tea,
The white flesh of a soft-boiled egg
    trembling on the tip of a teaspoon.
For Mercurius Duplex is a cockroach now
    hiding in a green pepper.
When the pepper is cut, he escapes, scuttling
    behind the bread bin. But we are careful, for we know
To fondle the reptile is to be bitten by it.
    So, to soothe the hubbub in our heads, we chant,
Lumen Christi gloriose resurgentis
    dissipet tenebras cordis et mentis.

The Scribe in the Scriptorium

I

I want nothing, yet lack everything,
   The writer's hell.
Just as a poet chooses words
   to release people from the tyranny of words,
So I must return to the genius loci
   who first taught me the sacred language.
I light a fire. I sit with a book. I contemplate
   the indescribable silence
Preparing me for the unknown,
   the pure labour of a poem.
Smiling does not come easily to me
   but when the work is over
I am a smile
   as wide as repletion itself.

II

I sip the wine of the kingdom
   in the sacramental economy.
I study the sacred sciences
   in the synod of the just.
But in regard to death
   the pathos of the human
Is shrouded in doubt.
   Wisdom is a word
Which cannot be eradicated,
   but what of the knowledge of truth
In the authentic magisterium
   when the sacred page lays bare
Unquenchable thirst for human dignity
   within the very depths of theology?

III

Who shows us the soul of the intellect?
   Faith to consummate hope?
Courage not to be calculated?
   Love of God to exhaust the incredulous?
Insight to serenade
   a camel waltzing through the eye of a needle?
Love of man to indicate
   the possibility of man?
Passion to revolutionize
   the common understanding of being?
Seriousness? Laughter? Our sense of the sacred?
   The triumph, in short, of intelligence
Over prejudice, stupidity, and cruelty?
   Of being loved over being degraded?

IV

The pulverization of the soul
   by the mechanical brutality of circumstance;
Tears in the eyes of many a mother;
   Pablo Picasso, that Spanish Hercules,
In twelve times twelve labours
   to uncover a valid sign;
The transference of hell
   from an underground ideogram of the mind
To the overground God-refuting horror
   (the deliberate enaction
Of a long and precise imagining):
   no, separation from Christ
Does not begin in the modern age
   but once upon a time . . .

V

The astonishing actions of the saviour God
   light up the time of the daystar,
The terra incognita of the galaxies.
   The burning bush of the definitive theophany
Lights up the time of the promises;
   the remnant of Israel; the poor of the people.
In the fullness of time, the Suffering Servant,
   hallowed human inhumed, unkillable in kind,
Walks on the waves of a sea of light
   brighter than the sun.
Prudence, the charioteer of the virtues,
   erects the shade of a tender conscience,
A giant awning, to observe the heat
   smelting truth from dross.

VI

What is the sign of a transcendent
   character in a person?
Why do wisdom and a person meet
   parched by the same thirst in the same heat?
Why are history and prayer such intimate bedfellows?
   On every page of the book of history
A trace of the inscrutable imprints itself.
   Contemplation is the gaze of faith
But the groaning of the ages remains.
   We pray as if everything depended on God
Yet work as if everything depended on us.
   What can we say but we are haunted?
You shall be holy,
   for I the Lord your God am holy.

VII

My faith is my philosophy of history.
   To sacralize history is to love
The wisdom to be found in it
   if any. Adrift in a world grown too large,
All independence gone,
   what is this psychological malaise
Which craves the cult of religious faith?
   Worse than loneliness, ennui,
That profound malady of the spirit,
   attacks through a form of madness,
Odium humani generis, hatred of the human race,
   because the world is odious.
As Marcion of Pontus knew, it's full
   of flies, fleas, and fevers.

VIII

Constantine called Christianity
   the struggle for deathlessness.
To this end, the pontifex maximus,
   the supreme bridge-maker,
Linked the Romanitas of the Greco-Romans
   to the holy spirit of the Byzantines.
Those who minded to be free of death
   confessed one Adonai, one Kyrios, one Dominus,
One Lord of the Tetragrammaton, YaHWeH.
   The concordat of faith, empire, and emperor
Constituted the state symphonia
   of the Spaniard Theodosius.
As the citizens of the state grew fat,
   the militia christi in the desert thinned.

IX

Justinian's great church, Hagia Sophia,
    meant Christ, the holy wisdom to be found
Deposited in the church: the sacred words
    written down as the word of God
Under the influence of the holy spirit.
    Tortured by physical pain
Extirpating the integrity of the body;
    tormented by mental dread
Of once and for all ceasing to be:
    the dignity of the person
Cowers before the dominance of death.
    The cleric responds with the revelation
Of the word, radioactive within
    the sacred deposit.

X

God is aware of the mind of man
    in the exact ratio
Man is aware of the mind of God.
    Irenaeus called this divine pedagogy.
The congregation of the conscious preaches
    the fate of man is whipped by its furies
Through the very hell on earth of death,
    a fireproof seed whipped by the wind
Blown through the gates of the all-creating furnace.
    Is the fate of man reducible to the seed?
Beyond the white waterfall of fire within
    the im- and the -passibility of the word teaches
Here is the water in which lambs may walk
    and elephants swim.

The Teraphim of Trash

I

I came to the Cenacle covered by a dome
    studded with sapphires, sparkling
Blue, celestial brilliance. Just as a sculptor
    cries out, slapping a slab of marble,
'What fantastic beauty sleeps in here?'
    so I saw the skeleton
Of a woman, her bones snow white,
    walking towards me
Simulating authenticity,
    the ghost of a heroine from the future
Not the past. Wearing a woollen pallium,
    she colligated such passion within me
With her own, I could have sworn
    she was a living woman, and more.

II

As my enthusiasm prospered,
    she took on flesh,
Her black pallium (lined with fur,
    clasped by an iron buckle)
Resting on her shoulders. Naked beneath,
    she bloomed before my eyes,
Suspending disbelief with a regal
    disdain of popular ogling;
Before reverting to the skeleton
    equally alive. And so she oscillated.
I saw the power of the spirit
    informing her. The air darkened.
The apparition vanished. By then I knew
    I was on holy ground.

III

Big with wonder, scop of the fistula,
   I move in Messinias in the spring.
Poems on the secrets of the air
   leap from the gorges of the Neda
Into the permanence of sound.
   In the ecclesia domestica, I drink
The hydromel of happiness, the chiparo of cheer.
   An Attic white lekythos,
Holding the ashes of my parents
   like the incandescence of radium,
Topples to a pillow
   on which my own children
Dream, to wake, to rest,
   to grow on holy ground.

IV

Mayflies in the blue air of the morning:
   I see DNA on wings,
The birdman of the minimalist,
   coming into being
And leaving it at leisure.
   Junkyard palaces, hillocks of dead cars,
The teraphim of trash,
   do not detain me. I see
Majesty is not so majestic
   as my athlete in her pallium,
Her flesh as fresh and fit and fair
   as the fish in the river Alpheos.
I observe the Pythagorean maxim,
   Follow God.

V

Naked yourself, follow a naked Christ:
  The spectre of Jerome
Urges me like a nagging nanny,
  his barkhard face soaked with tears,
His sex like a leather bottle in the frost:
  Be the cicada of the night.
Continuity. Ingenuity. Research.
  A flock of sheep gongles through the village.
The sky is swept by a whoosh of wind.
  The unimpeachable sea
Scatters the remnants of my mind.
  Of the seven gifts of the holy spirit,
Sapientia is the first,
  Timor Domini the seventh.

VI

A man must hunt in search of his life.
  She is Sapientia. She teaches
Terror of God's the beginning of wisdom.
  Men drown, a foul agnostic welter
In Stygian seas of mind, dead spawn of dead fish
  floating through the ocean.
The cursèd lust for gold, companionship
  deeper than the grave –
Lightning flashes on Mount Ithome.
  I see it. The maker's weird
(Wanderer, rider of the storm) wonders,
  Why are the sacred stones demolished,
Like that Sumerian fragment which says,
  A righteous soul will never die?

VII

She fondles the queen's lyre, inlaid with pink
   limestone, mother of pearl, lapis lazuli,
Set to last in bitumen. She strikes the strings.
   I lift her obsidian dagger,
Volcanic glass mined on Milos,
   pitchblack, translucent at the edges.
Its silver handle is alive with gold
   lions, a rhinoceros on wings.
Can the burnt out lamp on her tungsten table
   catch fire from the light of the sun?
Mobiles of carnelian fruit, haematite leaves,
   vibrate to the music. My cup is hollowed agate
Holding the purity of ruby wine.
   Let's have a drop, she sings.

VIII

I am drunk on her wine. No one
   will ever find me sober again.
For the flash in the eyes of my lyrical lady,
   sharper than steel, pierces
The scrutiny of a laser, exposing
   its callow operator in a futile skirmish.
As Protagoras did not quip,
   Woman is the measure of all things.
And so, to the queen's lyre, she sings,
   Because we cannot understand
The devouring dogs of death, we die ourselves.
   Speak! if you have wisdom!
Who is insulted by the precedence of God?
   Justicia immortalis est.

IX

The lyrebird of futurity
 flies to the house of the dead.
Here is the hole where people sit in darkness;
 dust is their drink, clay their meat.
Clothed like birds, wings like overcoats,
 they see no light, they sit in darkness.
Let us honour the house of the dead, she says,
 the kings and crooks of the earth,
The crowns and crowds on fungoid hooks
 petrified to the rock. The iron age
Rets. The jazz age drips with sentiment.
 Cultural gruel slips from the stalactites.
Rain has the power, she says, to equal
 the resurrection of the dead.

X

The wider he opens the auricles of his heart,
 the wider the molten bdellium on fire
Pours on the floor. O listen, dear friends!
 Smothered to death by cassia?
Zapped to a zero by zealots of the state?
 Easy to miss the tempora christi
At the turn of a civilization.
 Bede, the candle of the church,
Illuminates the gloom, toils the tortuous
 track to the throb of the ventricles.
Language is the house of the living, she says,
 the poet its signature. Bede will guide you
Up rivers of fire towards it, through
 the abysmal depths of human character.

The Argosy of Faith

I

I lie in the tomb of my sins,
    the babel of a distracted mind,
Like my belly and my sex,
    usurpers of all reason. Yet I am aboard
The argosy of faith, the valiant ones
    nurses beside me,
The giddiness of my seasickness
    fouling the ancient stains
Vomited around me.
    For I believe in love, when it tells me
The stars are not pure in God's sight
    nor I. For love inclines us,
It unites us, for love occurs
    through the open infilling of our reason.

II

I will be the pattern of all patience
    making my ship of worth a worship,
Searching the horrible steep, the extreme verge,
    the cruel, the delicate stratagem.
A Christian is not born but made.
    Surfeited to vanity by the musk of wine,
Stupefied to nausea by the flesh of quails,
    a rotund paunch rarely breeds fine thoughts.
And fear of ridicule makes ambition hijack
    the spirit of reverence,
The abiding penalty of an ancient malediction.
    May the cradlings of a newborn faith
Grant me a lover's humility.
    I am mourning the dead of the world.

III

My heart is numb, my hands tremble,
  my eyes are full of tears, my voice falters.
I can think of nothing but your death.
  What can I, my poor soul, what can I do?
Where has it gone your beautiful face?
  Where is it now your dignified body?
Grief is like a lily withering in the wind,
  grief is like a violet trampled in the mud.
Diverse extreme and sore calamities,
  the bells of a wedding, the solo lamentation:
Like dust on the face of the earth,
  we are the playthings of the wind.
Is there anything more miserable than man,
  loving his life to learn he must lose it?

IV

As soon as we are born we are dying,
  feasting beside our fellows begging bread,
Reading the unrolled scrolls of parchment,
  the gold leaf lettering,
The manuscripts embossed with moonstones,
  gold on the ceilings, gold on the walls,
Gold on the capitals of the pillars,
  the dying at the door
Naked, hungry, poor.
  Where is the courage as conspicuous
In sorrow as in war?
  Words weep, language buckles.
Like dust on the face of the earth,
  we are the playthings of the wind.

V

Weave creels of reed, baskets of osier.
　　Hoe and dig the earth. Sow cabbages in rows.
Channel the river water down. Make hives for bees.
　　Graft the trees with buds and slips.
An ass on the road makes for an inn
　　when weary. Where will I find
A language capable of rendering
　　religious apprehension of the world?
O power of divine fire! O strange energy!
　　With what fervour and what zeal
Do I read the coherent codices,
　　the mellifluous manuscripts,
Riveted to the uncreated light
　　shining on the slopes of Mount Tabor!

VI

O mighty soul within so weak a body!
　　Death was dead when life was dead on the tree!
Alphabets of ivory and boxwood
　　spell out the magic springtime of the sacred story.
Paul, you are mad.
　　Too much learning has driven you mad,
Said Porcius Festus of Caesarea.
　　A God-shaped emptiness,
Like the deep receptacle of the blank page,
　　directs the reaction of my judgment.
My faith is a force which acts
　　out of the very build of my soul.
In every rank and condition of life,
　　I champion the dignity of man.

VII

Because I cannot advance
   beyond the scope of my wit,
The inescapable terminus of death
   teaches what Plato taught: to live
Is the chance to negotiate with death.
   I follow the prophetic way, but yet
I part with my attitudes less easily
   than the treacherous with truth. I see,
Galloping through the Caspian Gates
   past the distant Sea of Asov, the Huns
Lifting their swords to decapitate
   smiling children, who smile because
They suspect nothing. Am I, too, credulous
   before the malignancy of fate?

VIII

The Armenians have stuck to their vows.
   The Huns have learnt the psalter.
The frosts of Scythia, home to the fierce tribes
   of the Massagetae, warmed to the fires of faith.
Ruddy, flaxen-haired Thracians
   pitched tent churches among their many armies.
Everywhere
   the bones of our ancestors turned to faith.
Under the weight of the freight of the dead,
   who cries out in the silence of the sky
Rolling overhead? I look around.
   The grass is cadmium green,
The sun trapped in a familiar garden.
   Who are the slaughtered innocents unborn?

IX

The Archprophet of the Epiclesis
   measures the malice of Moloch,
Whose odium theologicum was never so rich,
   whose alethiology was never so poor,
Whose stiff-necked alembicated eyes
   suck back to hell
Between a rock and a hard place:
   'Keep shtum, my dears, the schola cantorum,
The matris fons, the osculatorium,
   the illapse of the holy spirit itself,
Dissolve in the imaginations
   of vacuous populists. The rumour mill, like war,
Destroys the past. Those who laugh with the devil
   do not rejoice with Christ.'

X

I renounce the filius iniquitatis.
   O dazzling candour of the lux eterna,
O tower of strength, O ivory tower,
   desire of eternal hills, like a whisper
Fading in the faintest of breezes,
   do I hear the Paráclitos voice
An intelligible utterance of God?
   Holy the heart on which we hang our hope.
My life has been snatched like a sparrow
   out of the beak of a golden eagle.
Like the morning star among the clouds,
   like the sun shining on the dome of St Paul's,
Like a cypress tree reaching for the sky, rooted to the earth,
   so is my God among the derelict.

Against the Deadening of the Mind

I

Rock-graven epigram, madrigal of fact:
    who is so hubristic to believe
Understanding ours? The deeper in we go
    the more we learn the ecstasy to know.
Nothing is so risky as success.
    Forget dependence and our very mass
Hangs on a hair: the deadening strikes.
    Those without love are already dead.
If grace of God will let me, I shall coin
    paten, plate, and corrody in gold
Out of the mintage of antiquity.
    Carts full of apples shall supply
Silent haulage of cathedral stone.
    O God of truth keep my story straight.

II

Rome, departed glory moan,
    weep your luminaries gone.
It's no use locking the stable door
    after flogging the dead horse
That bolted. What holy poet kept
    locked in obscurity,
Malevolence of fame, slenderness of luck,
    his straw, till freedom kills him,
Sings, O Marranos, O Sanbenitos, come,
    pronounce the word most terrible to hear
In anamnesis of the true irenics?
    Samarra, mate, that is what it is.
The black cotton scapular you wear
    relaxing after Mass burning at the stake.

III

Pornocracy satanic to betray
   the holy word knows the holy spirit
Never dies.
   What better then than mortifying it?
Step straight up. Dress the part. Conceal
   you move as a monster. Cry to heaven.
Suck the teat that feeds you. Bite it off.
   To labour is to pray. But not for you
Lounging in the triple concupiscence:
   sex and envy shooting up on pride.
O superstar and senator of lies
   you pirouette on platinum, on Paul.
Luxurious episcopus, you sip
   no toxin but the history of sin.

IV

Wilful word-hip poetpops inspire
   ahistoricity to make
Bald painted coconuts:
   history in a nutshell repeats itself
First as tragedy then again as tragedy.
   Thus, we may advance
The philosophic vice of the sloshed
   is solipsism. Churn the painted pates
Round and round a dustbin with the dead
   drooping Jesus. Establish each a place
Daily in the palanquins of power
   consubstantial with the bloody news . . .
O holy souls, research the starry city
   seen from a plane, the beating brain.

V

There is no sound like London in the spring,
    the River Lee unlost in it, singing.
Visible map of invisible God,
    who walks the bank, talking to the swans
Under the willows where the grass grows green?
    Man is what he's worth in sight of God,
And no more, he says. The swans do not reply,
    voting with their feet, being
Identical with beatitude to behold
    such a lean and strenuous fellow
At one with the willows. They hear his
    strange cry of ecstasy
Thrill with wonder
    the heart of Hackney Marsh.

VI

Silenced by articulated rapture,
    no one blest with happiness will say
Why I myself in poverty and pain,
    aching heart in ice cold rooms alone,
Wasted whole winters, if not for him.
    Grievous and burdensome to myself,
In darkness and insecure,
    I watched the dark waters, obscene and afflictive,
No one walks or echoes in the night.
    The fingers of God had ravished me,
The hands of the Elohim, but the river
    was black with blood, fingers and hands
Clutched at the riverbanks, O monstrous horror,
    fixed to flow through my veins.

VII

I turn, I return, I repent
   to the green olive tree, fair with fruit,
Jerusalem.
   The holy road is always clear and pure,
Like the tender-hearted seraphic Assisian,
   whose blinding tears have cleansed his inner eye,
Who looks at God not at himself.
   Like the harvest moon shining on the rooftops of London,
Like lilies trembling on the banks of the Thames,
   like cups of hammered gold
Inlaid with malachite and topaz,
   like the majesty of Saint Paul's Cathedral
Rising through the dawn of a new millennium,
   so are we in the hands of our Maker.

VIII

The People of the Book,
   a trinity of man,
No common God mistook
   before the Book began.
Prophets of them all
   know all creation small
Compared to the Creator.
   Worlds piled high in blood
Of people slaughtered people,
   all implied in all,
Do not drown the scale
   nor drench the tall Creator.
The Lamb of God, I saw,
   limps silent to the slaughter.

IX

Whom God enriches, no,
  nobody makes poor.
Who pity, then, the poor,
  enrich the richest God.
As gold and silver try
  the superbowl of fire,
The souls of Christ hold hands
  behind him.
I cry you mercy, Lord.
  I cry you mercy, Lord.
Faith, he says, is fixed,
  the furnace not so firm.
His genii arrive.
  The Lord God knows his own.

X

No honey, no, no spice,
  exalts like altar wine.
Thirst itself gives thirst
  a taste of the divine.
An eagle stole a coal
  burning under mine.
He's charcoal in his nest.
  Who values more than gold
And silver, virtue, feels
  the furnace not so firm,
The thickest sharpest steels
  melting in the bowl,
The honest Christian soul
  voyaging to God.

Damnatio Memoriae

The Exegesis

Dear Daniel & Xanthi,

The notes to this poem form an exegesis, or an explanation in detail. I have written it because it did not seem reasonable to present the poem without an attempt, no matter how poor, to explain its references and its sources.

They say poems should not come with notes. However, this is not a universal axiom. Take the nursery rhyme:

Mary, Mary, quite contrary,
How does your garden grow?
With silver bells and cockle shells,
And little maids all in a row.

Mary is Mary Tudor, Queen of England and wife of Philip II of Spain. Mary is contrary because she is trying to reverse the changes made to the church in England by Henry VIII: she is trying to revert Protestant Reformation England to Catholic Counter-Reformation England. Her garden is the realm of England. The silver bells are the bells sounded in the Transubstantiation of the Catholic Mass. The cockle shells are the characteristic signs or badges worn by Catholics on pilgrimage to Santiago de Compostella in northwest Spain. The little maids in a row are Catholic priests dressed up (as it were) like women.

You will agree, I think, that to know this nursery rhyme without understanding the references is to know it in innocence. By understanding the references, we add to the innocence the knowledge of historical experience. Or take:

Ring a ring of roses,
A pocketful of posies,
A-tishoo, a-tishoo,
We all fall down.

The roses refer to the characteristic rash which appears on a person at the first sign of plague. The rash is circular, therefore a ring of roses. A pocketful of posies refers to the sweet-smelling pomander sniffed to ward off the stench of the plague. A-tishoo, a-tishoo signify the plague transmitted in the droplets of the sneezes.

So I have made this exegesis to make what is opaque, transparent. Poetry – nursery rhymes are its nursery slopes – can be obstinate in that what is clear to the poet may be opaque to the rest of us. In such circumstances, exegesis can be useful because it helps to show why one word was chosen rather than another. Each word before you has been carefully considered in order to perform a precise and particular duty. If I could have used a more ordinary word, in any given case, I would have done.

I have frequently chosen an English word which is a translation of a word originally written or spoken in another language, such as Hebrew, Aramaic (the language of Christ), Greek, Latin, Arabic, Persian, Welsh, Anglo-Saxon, Middle Dutch, German, 18th-century American, or 20th-century French, for example.

Quite a few of the words in the original languages are to be found in poems. They say poetry is what is lost in translation. However, in making this English poem, my concern in choosing a word, and considering the order in which the words are placed, was to convey not an original poetry but an original meaning – or something close to it.

My aim, therefore, has been to make a poem in the English language whose meaning has its sources in many languages in the Semitic and Indo-European groups of languages. Of the languages I have mentioned, Hebrew, Aramaic, and Arabic belong to the Semitic group; the rest, like English, belong to the Indo-European.

You will notice that without the exegesis there is quite a lot which is incomprehensible. In the writing of a poem which is about what has been forgotten, *damnatio memoriae: erased from memory*, this is, perhaps, inevitable. With an exegesis, it may be, there is at least the possibility of comprehension. So the exegesis is like the answers at the back of a school book. It shows, amongst other things, the actual form of the words in the sources cited, translated or otherwise, which were used, and sometimes changed, to provide the words and therefore the voices of the poem.

If you want further details of works cited, such as particular editions, editors, original languages, translators, page numbers of the citations, and so on, just let me know.

Your Father.

Damnatio Memoriae

I

(1) *For the arrows of the Almighty are in me; / my spirit drinks their poison; / the terrors of God are arrayed against me.* Job 6:4, *c.* 400 BC, N[ew] R[evised] S[tandard] V[ersion] of the Bible]. Works cited in the Bible are not in italics.

(2) *Truly, you are a God who hides himself.* Isaiah 45:15, NRSV, *c.* 540 BC.

(3) *the Wadi of the Willows.* Isaiah 15:7, NRSV. Wadi is an Arabic word for a river valley.

(4) *under every green tree.* Isaiah 57:5, Jeremiah 2:20, Ezekiel 6:13, NRSV. The phrase was used by the prophets to signify places where gods were worshipped by gentiles and Hebrew apostates.

(5) *lost / In loss it self.* John Milton (1608–1674), *Paradise Lost*, bk. 1, 525–6.

(6) *deep as Sheol or high as heaven.* Isaiah 7:11, NRSV. Sheol, a word of unknown derivation often found in the old testament, signifies the underworld or hades or hell.

(7) *I will sing praise to my God while I have being.* Psalm 104:33, NRSV, first half of 1st millennium BC.

(8) *eulogizing the abyss of divine charity.* Thomas Aquinas (*c.* 1225–74), Dominican theologian, 'Sermon on the Body of the Lord'.

(9) *Moan therefore, mortal; moan with breaking heart and bitter grief.* Ezekiel 21:6, NRSV, *c.* 590 BC.

II

(1) *I believe, that the notion of God is essential to the human mind; that it is called forth into distinct consciousness principally by the conscience.* Samuel Taylor Coleridge (1772–1834), 'Confessio Fidei'.

(2) *God's hand is his power working visible things invisibly.* Augustine (354–430), bishop of Hippo, *The City of God*.

(3) *Who dare calumniate the duty of holy love?* Augustine, *The City of God*.

(4) *the union caused by love is closer than that which is caused by knowledge.* Thomas Aquinas, 'Of the Effects of Love', *Summa Theologica*.

(5) *that all-dividing and all-effective divine power, which cannot be made but makes.* Augustine, *The City of God*.

(6) *You [God] cause wine to gladden the human heart.* Psalm 104:14–15, NRSV.

(7) *Things are beautiful by the indwelling of God.* Thomas Aquinas, 'Exposition of the Psalms'.

(8) *The wine-halls crumble; their wielders lie / bereft of bliss . . . / Alas, bright cup!* Anglo-Saxon poet, *c.* 7th century?, 'The Wanderer', translated by Michael Alexander.

III

(1) *A few whose Eyes were piercing, and whose Foreheads spoke Thought.* Samuel Taylor Coleridge, 'On the Origin of Evil'.

(2) *O Truth, homeland of wanderers and the end of exile!* Bernard (1090–1153), abbot of Clairvaux, 'Sermon 50 on the Song of Songs'.

(3) *Better that scandal erupt than that the truth be abandoned.* Gregory the Great (*c.* 540–604), pope from 590, 'Exposition of Ezekiel'.

(4) *the consecrated senses of the holy man.* Bonaventura (*c.* 1217–1274), Franciscan theologian, *The Life of Saint Francis*.

(5) *Empires crumble: religion alone endures.* Jacques-Bénigne Bossuet (1627–1704), bishop of Meaux, *Discours sur l'Histoire Universelle*.

(6) *Who will unlock for me the mystery of the mutability of God?* Bernard of Clairvaux, 'Sermon 74 on the Song of Songs'.

(7) *His speech was as a burning fire, penetrating the secrets of the heart.* Bonaventura, *The Life of Saint Francis*.

IV

(1) *Take this pain from me, for I cannot bear it.* Margery Kempe (*c.* 1373–*c.* 1438), visionary, *The Book of Margery Kempe*.

(2) *Your prayers are burning me.* Pseudo-Bede, 'Homilies 2', cited in *Ancrene Wisse (Guide for Anchoresses)*, *c.* 1235.

(3) *The glory of Christ's Church is the life of the solitaries.* Isaac of Nineveh (d. *c.* 700), monastic writer.

(4) *Monks are the sinews and foundations of the church.* Theodore of Studios (759–826), monastic reformer.

(5) *Money is the sinews of war.* Gaius Licinius Mucianus (d. *c.* 77), governor of Syria.

(6) *The world is all that is the case.* Ludwig Wittgenstein (1889–1951), German philosopher, *Tractatus Logico-Philosophicus*.

(7) *The world itself is God's greatest miracle.* Augustine, 'On the Arrival of Saint Stephen's Relics'.

(8) *For Holy Church shall be shaken at the world's sorrow, anguish, and tribulation, just as men shake a cloth in the wind.* Julian of Norwich (*c.* 1342–*c.* 1416), *Revelations of Divine Love*.

(9) *the lectio divina.* The sacred books used by monks in their meditations.

(10) *So that a cockle-fish may as soon crowd the ocean into its narrow shell, as vain man ever comprehend the decrees of God.* William Beveridge (1637–1708), bishop of St Asaph in north Wales, *Ecclesia Anglicana Ecclesia Catholica*.

V

(1) *steeped in the depravity of the Arian heresy.* Gregory of Tours (*c.* 538–94), *The History of the Franks*. Arius (d. 336), denied the full divinity of Christ. The orthodox view of the church, established by the General Council at Nicaea in 325, held that the Father and the Son were co-equal or consubstantial or (in Greek) homo-ousios.

(2) *The whole world was suddenly lit by the sunshine of the saving word.* Eusebius (*c.* 260–*c.* 340), bishop of Caesarea, *The History of the Church*.

(3) *the Holy Word of God is not only laid on the shelf, but is almost mouldered away with dust and moths.* Martin Luther (1483–1546), preface to *Theologia Germanica* by a priest of the Teutonic Order, late 14th century.

(4) *For we are the temple of the living God.* The Second Letter of Paul to the Corinthians 6:16, NRSV.

(5) *Churches make no man holy, but men make churches holy.* John Tauler (d. 1361), German Dominican, at the consecration of Cologne Cathedral, 26 September 1357.

(6) *The glory of God is a living man; and the life of man is the vision of God.* Ireneaus (*c.* 130–*c.* 200), bishop of Lyons, *Refutation of All Heresies*.

VI

(1) *the good angel touches the soul sweetly, lightly and gently, like a drop of water going into a sponge.* Ignatius Loyola (*c.* 1491–1556), founder of the Jesuits, *Spiritual Exercises*.

(2) *no beast on the face of the earth is as ferocious as the enemy of human nature.* Ignatius Loyola, *Spiritual Exercises*.

(3) *sanctity shows 'shorn of its rays' through the black fog of universal utilitarianism.* Francis Thompson (1859–1907), English poet, *Saint Ignatius Loyola*.

(4) *The Basque beggar saint, / with a furnace under his arm.* Ignatius Loyola was a Basque who lived for years as a beggar in the course of educating himself. He embodies here the spirit of education, which the Jesuits brought to the forefront of the church. He also embodies, therefore, the mistakes committed by himself, the Jesuits, and the church as a whole. He carries *a furnace under his arm*, a furnace from a deathcamp because, as the spirit of education, he walks towards us *in the black fog of the Black Forest* to teach us, *dictates to me,* the origins of the deathcamps in the culture of anti-judaism and antisemitism as old as Christianity. This is death by mass murder on an industrial scale.

(5) *the unshakeable champion of true belief.* Francis Thompson's description of Ignatius Loyola.

(6) *As I write I wipe away my tears.* Gregory of Tours, writing about the death of children in a plague, *The History of the Franks*. This is death by disease.

(7) *The tears roll down my face, and though I steel my courage I cannot hide the pain which I suffer.* Jerome (*c.* 345–420), biblical scholar, letter to Heliodorus on the death of their friend Nepotianus. This is death by natural causes.

VII

(1) *The discipline of silence is the nurse of speech.* Gregory the Great, 'Homily on Ezekiel'.

(2) *Reason compels understanding to see.* Anselm of Bec (*c.* 1033–1109), who became archbishop of Canterbury, *Monologion*. In *Proslogion*, he wrote his ontological proof of the existence of God.

(3) *The sons of wisdom are the church of the just.* Derived from: 'The multitude of the wise is the salvation of the world.' The Wisdom of Solomon 6:24, NRSV, by an Alexandrian Jew, 1st-2nd century BC.

(4) *The madness of the godless is more bitter than death.* Athanasius (*c.* 296–373), bishop of Alexandria, 'First Letter to the Monks', conflating Ecclesiastes 7:25 *foolishness is madness* and 7:26 *I found more bitter than death the woman who is a trap*. NRSV.

(5) *The mind seeks its own good, though like a drunkard it cannot find the path home.* Boethius (*c.* 480–*c.* 524), *The Consolation of Philosophy*.

(6) *He [God] remembered that they were but flesh, / a wind that passes and does not come again.* Psalm 78:39, NRSV.

(7) *We must all die; we are like water spilled on the ground, which cannot be gathered up.* 2 Samuel 14:14, *c.* 6th century BC, NRSV.

(8) *You will forget your misery; / you will remember it as waters that have passed away.* Job 11:16, NRSV.

(9) *Wine is bottled poetry.* Painted on a beam in the Barley Mow pub in Limehouse, London.

(10) *Wheat is holy speech.* Rabanus Maurus (*c.* 780–856), Carolingian poet, abbot of Mainz.

(11) *For the bread of charity is holy bread.* Francis of Assisi (1181–1226), founder of the Franciscan Order. *The Mirror of Perfection*, compiled by Friar Leo, 1318.

VIII

(1) *The grace of generosity returns to its originator.* Ambrose (*c.* 339–97), bishop of Milan, 'On Naboth'. Naboth's vineyard was coveted by king Ahab and his wife Jezebel. They bore false witness against him, and had him stoned to death. Naboth is the type of the poor robbed to make the rich richer. 1 Kings 21:1–16.

(2) *Reason in man is rather like God in the world.* Thomas Aquinas, 'On Kingship'.

(3) *No man truly has joy unless he lives in love.* Thomas Aquinas, 'On the Two Precepts'.

(4) *We cannot love and not pity.* Julian of Norwich, *Revelations of Divine Love.*

(5) *For no man that ever confessed Christ could lose him amongst all the torments.* Augustine, *The City of God.*

(6) *It is God, the mind's true wealth, that makes us happy.* Augustine, *The City of God.*

(7) *the prima philosophia.* The study of fundamental principles. In this study, Aristotle identifies three sciences: mathematics, natural science, and theology. For him, theology comes first: 'It is this first science of theology that we must prefer to all other kinds of contemplation.' The prime mover is a fundamental principle. The prime mover activates thought which in turn causes all movement and all physical processes. So to be able to activate thought is to be able to activate life. God is that ability. As such, Aristotle asserts 'God is a supreme and eternal living being.' Aristotle (384–322 BC), *The Metaphysics.* See Maimonides below.

(8) *Now if God be wisdom, as truth and scripture testify, then a true philosopher is a lover of God.* Augustine, *The City of God.*

(9) *The study of truth is called philosophy.* Aristotle, *The Metaphysics.*

IX

(1) *Maimonides* (1138–1204), known as Rambam from his full name Rabbi Moses ben Maimon. 'The most fundamental of all principles and the basis of all learning is the knowledge of the existence of the Supreme Being.' Cited in his *The [613] Commandments,* 1990 edition. His work seeks to reconcile Jewish revelation and Aristotelian reason. It influenced theologian and scientist Albert the Great (*c.* 1195–1280), and Thomas Aquinas; and through them the church. The words spoken by Maimonides are cited in *The Jewish Encyclopedia,* 1903.

(2) *For who is competent, however torrential the flow of his eloquence, to unfold all the miseries of this life?* Augustine, *The City of God.*

(3) *The truth is that the more holy a man is, and the deeper his longing for holiness, the more abundant is his weeping when he prays.* Augustine, *The City of God.*

(4) *from all unbegun eternity.* Augustine, *The City of God.*

X

(1) *Holy art thou, whom nature hath not formed.* 'Hymns to the All-Father', *The Divine Pymander [Shepherd] of Hermes Trismegistos,* author and date unknown, but familiar to the church fathers in the 1st–3rd centuries.

(2) *As everlasting foundations upon a solid rock, so the commandments of God in the heart of a holy woman.* Cited in *Saint Andrew Daily Missal,* Bruges, 1956. *Daily Missal.*

(3) *the Word is clothed in flesh as the candle-flame is cupped in wax.* Guerric of Igny (d. 1157), Cistercian monk, 'The First Sermon for the Purification'.

(4) *Every creature is to God as the air to the sun that lights it.* Thomas Aquinas, *Summa Theologica.*

(5) *poltroons.* A poltroon is a craven, pusillanimous coward.

(6) *popeholy.* Pretending to holiness and piety. Hypocrites.

(7) *The person who gathers virtues and does not include humility is like one who carries dust in the wind.* Gregory the Great, 'Homily on the Gospels'.

(8) *Those souls who close their eyes that they may see.* Dionysius the Pseudo-Areopagite, *c.* 500, theologian, *Mystical Theology*.

(9) *The land of the living is cut off by a deep divide from this land of the dying.* Guerric of Igny, 'The Second Sermon for Advent'.

Columbarium: An Eclogue from the Auvergne

I

(1) *The central personage in alchemical lore [is] the spirit of Mercury, alias Hermes Trismegistos, Thrice Greatest Hermes. In alchemy Mercury is the all-embracing personality, uniting above and below, good and evil, base and sublime. He is elusive, ambivalent and with multiple meanings, which is why he is called Mercurius duplex. He symbolises both the lowest prima materia and the highest lapis philosophorum . . . Christ, lacking the dimension of evil, was inferior as a symbol of the Self [in Jung's view] to the lapis or philosopher's stone. This was what enabled us to see [in Jung] the superiority of Mercury as symbol, for he was Mercurius utriusque capax (Mercury capable of both), a symbol of ambivalence superior to his divided and alienated Christian counterparts, the Holy Ghost as summum bonum (greatest good) and Satan as summum malum (the greatest evil).* Frank McLynn, *Carl Gustav Jung*, 1996.

(2) The Mercurius is *superliterate* because of his higher qualities.

(3) *The paterfamilias of our ecclesia.* The patriarch, the father of the family, the abbot of our abbey or church. The model here is the Cistercian monastery in the Auvergne, La Chaise Dieu, founded by Robert of Turlande in 1044.

(4) *the codex.* The manuscript volume from which the abbot reads aloud the boastings of the Mercurius.

II

(1) *minds that have lost philosophical sensitivity.* Stanley L. Jaki, *God and the Cosmologists*, 1989. Jaki attacked the Copenhagen school of physicists, represented by Niels Bohr and Werner Heisenberg, on the grounds that because they did *good science*, this meant they thought they could get away with *doing philosophy badly*. 'They rejected in the name of quantum mechanics any concern about reality as such, that is, about ontology, as unscientific and unphilosophical, to be avoided at all costs in physics.' Jaki's fundamental principle is revelation: God as 'He Who Is or ontology incarnate.'

(2) *The fool hath said in his heart, There is no God.* Psalm 14:1, K[ing] J[ames] V[ersion].

III

(1) *the mind at home in the spacious circuits of her musing.* John Milton, 'The Reason of Church Government Urged Against Prelaty', 1642.

IV

(1) *Poetry is the art of uniting pleasure with truth, by calling imagination to the help of reason.* Dr Samuel Johnson (1709–84), 'Milton', *Lives of the Poets.*

(2) *the scriptorium.* The writing room in which monks illuminated and copied manuscripts.

(3) *omphalos.* Greek for navel. The sacred stone in the temple of Apollo at Delphi symbolising the centre of the world. The fountain in the poem serves this purpose.

(4) *scholastici.* Latin for teachers and students of rhetoric. The monks are like the medieval scholastics, the Schoolmen of the Schools of theology and philosophy.

(5) *frying / on the gridirons of the Mercurius.* Having trouble explaining the origin of evil in a world created by a good God. The Mercurius, capable of both, has no such trouble. Attempting to square the Mercurius with orthodox theology.

V

(1) *For what is more wretched than envy?* Augustine, *The City of God.*

(2) *God is not a person, except in Christ.* Jacob Boehme (1575–1624), German cobbler and writer, *Mysterium Magnum.*

(3) *I continue my course with the precision and security of a sleepwalker.* Adolf Hitler, 1938.

(4) *the 'alchemystical' philosophers made the opposites and their union one of the chief objects of their work.* C. G. Jung (1875–1961), *Mysterium Coniunctionis.*

(5) *a vision is in the last analysis nothing less than a dream which has broken through into the waking state.* C. G. Jung, 'Transformation Symbolism in the Mass', *Psychology and Religion.*

(6) *Men are not intelligent, the gods are intelligent.* Heraclitus, *Herakleitos & Diogenes*, translated by Guy Davenport. *God is intelligence.* Irenaeus, *Refutation of All Heresies. Not an atom's weight in the heavens or the earth escapes Him.* Surah 34, 'Sheba', *The Koran*, dictated to Muhammad (*c.* 570–632). *The first author and mover of the universe is an intellect.* Thomas Aquinas, 'In What Consists the Office of a Wise Man', *Summa Contra Gentiles.*

(7) *a small river, gentle and clear, which like some women has the gift of perpetual grace.* Freda White, writer, *Three Rivers of France.*

VI

(1) *The sad ghost of Coleridge beckons to me from the shadows.* T. S. Eliot (1888–1965), *The Use of Poetry & the Use of Criticism.*

(2) *If I had a God I could understand, I would not understand him to be God.* Augustine, 'Sermon 117'.

VII

(1) *the secret music of the intelligence.* Jacques Maritain (1882–1973), French philosopher, *Creative Intuition in Art & Poetry.*

(2) *Art is a virtue of the practical intellect.* Maritain, op. cit.

(3) *creative innocence is the paradise of poetic intuition.* Maritain, op. cit.

(4) *creative intuition may be at work in darkness and despairing agony.* Maritain, op. cit.

(5) *they know enough who know how to learn.* Henry Adams (1838–1918), American writer and historian, *The Education of Henry Adams.*

(6) *poetry has its source in the preconceptual life of the intellect.* Maritain, op. cit.

(7) *Tis that Zonulet of love, / Wherein all pleasures of the world are wove.* Robert Herrick (1591–1674), English poet, 'Upon Julia's Riband'. A zonulet is a small zone.

VIII

(1) *I turned colder than a Gallic winter . . . We were drowned in wine, Falerian at that . . . Right in the doorway lounged the porter in green clothes with a cherry-coloured belt, shelling peas in a silver dish . . . The rest of our party bellowed with laughter as I reassembled my nerves . . . Boys from Alexandria came pouring snow-cooled water over our hands . . . On the sideboard stood a donkey of Corinthian bronze, with olives carried in his panniers, white one side and black the other . . . A gridiron of silver was steaming with sausages . . . Ah ha, you scamper, you stare, you scurry about like a mouse in a chamber pot . . . My soul was in my nose, ready to be blown out . . . The free inspired spirit [of the poet] must leap headlong into dark mazes, into events where gods play their part, an incredible tumult of idea and significance.* Petronius Arbiter, 1st century, writer and arbiter of taste at the court of Nero, *The Satyricon*, translated by Jack Lindsay. I wanted in this stanza to fuse the voluptuous delights of *The Satyricon* with the ascetic rigours of a Cistercian monastery.

IX

(1) *Her body spoke with the irresistible language of beauty and invited me closer. There was a silence which was the sound of kissing endlessly beginning.* Petronius Arbiter, op. cit.

(2) *Imagination is like the sun. The sun has a light which is not tangible; but which, nevertheless, may set a house on fire.* Paracelsus (1493–1541), alchemist and physician.

(3) *penetralium.* The innermost part of a building, especially a shrine, sanctuary, or temple. *The penetralium of the word* is therefore the innermost part of the sanctity of language.

(4) *I . . . write all these Visions / to display Natures cruel holiness.* William Blake (1757–1827), *Milton a Poem*, Plate 36.

X

(1) *To fondle the reptile is to be bitten by it.* A proverb. O[xford] E[nglish] D[ictionary] under 'fondle'.

(2) Latin: *May the light of Christ in glory rising again / Dispel the darkness of heart and mind.* 'Easter Night', 'The Blessing of the Paschal Candle', *Daily Missal.*

The Scribe in the Scriptorium

I

(1) *the struggle for concentration . . . to return to that place where the Angel found you . . . I light the fire, I sit with my book, I contemplate, I delay endlessly, while drinking with all my senses that indescribable silence that frightened me as a child, but which loves me now, and more, is preparing me for I know not what, but I might guess, for my purest labour.* Rainer Maria Rilke (1875–1926), German poet, *Letters to Merline*.

(2) *Smiling does not come easily to me.* Rilke, op. cit.

II

(1) *wedding feast, wine of the kingdom, the Father's house, the heavenly Jerusalem, paradise.* Images of communion with God. *Catechism of the Catholic Church*, Veritas, Dublin, 1994. *Catechism*. The word 'catechism' is from Greek 'catechesis' meaning 'down' plus 'to sound'. Catechism is sounding down through time the sacred instruction. A parallel instruction is called in the orient 'the ear-whispered truths'.

(2) The 'divinity that shapes our ends, / Rough-hew them how we will' (William Shakespeare, 1564–1616, *Hamlet*) acts in a way appropriate to the age. It acts through the sacraments in what is traditionally called *the sacramental economy*.

(3) *the sacred sciences.* Detailed knowledge of the sacramental economy.

(4) *It is in regard to death that man's condition is most shrouded in doubt. Catechism.*

(5) *The first man did not know wisdom fully, / nor will the last one fathom her.* Ecclesiasticus, or the Wisdom of Jesus Son of Sirach 24:28, *c.* 190 BC. Sirach.

(6) *the authentic Magisterium.* The *OED* defines magisterium as (1) in alchemy: magisterium is from classical Latin meaning the office of a master. In medieval Latin it came to mean the philosopher's stone. 'This is the day, I am to perfect for him / The magisterium, our great worke, the stone.' Ben Jonson (1573–1637), English poet and dramatist, *The Alchemist*. (2) in Catholic theology: the magisterium is the teaching function of the church.

(7) *the 'study of the sacred page' should be the very soul of sacred theology. Catechism.*

(8) *The ferment of the Gospel has aroused and continues to arouse in the hearts of men an unquenchable thirst for human dignity.* 'Joy & Hope', *Vatican Council II: The Conciliar & Post Conciliar Documents*, Dublin, 1975. *Vatican II*.

III

(1) *It is easier for a camel to go through the eye of a needle, than for a rich man to enter into the kingdom of God.* The Gospel According to Matthew 19:24, KJV.

IV

(1) *Affliction is not a psychological state; it is a pulverization of the soul by the mechanical brutality of circumstances.* Simone Weil (1909–43), French writer, *Gateway to God*.

(2) *Seven times their number of the Saxons they slew.* / *There were tears in the eyes of many a mother.* Aneurin, Welsh poet, mid to late 6th century, 'Gododdin'.

(3) *Picasso . . . that Spanish Hercules . . . Behind his untiring inventiveness there is the desire to uncover a valid sign.* David Jones (1895–1974), poet and painter, preface to *The Anathémata.*

(4) *We made the son of Mary and his mother a sign to mankind.* Surah 23, 'The Believers'. *Only the unbelievers deny Our signs. Never have you [Muhammad] read a book before this, nor have you ever transcribed one with your right hand . . . To those who are endowed with knowledge it is an undoubted sign.* Surah 29, 'The Spider'. *The Koran.*

(5) *The concentration and death camps of the twentieth century, wherever they exist, under whatever regime, are* Hell *made immanent. They are the transference of Hell from below the earth to its surface. They are the deliberate enactment of a long, precise imagining.* George Steiner (b. 1929), scholar and critic, *In Bluebeard's Castle,* his emphasis.

(6) *Hell itself has for its fiercest flame the separation of the soul from God.* C. H. Spurgeon (1834–92), religious writer, *The Treasury of David,* exposition of Psalm 22:1, 'My God, my God, why has thou forsaken me?' cried out by Jesus on the cross, Mark 15:34, Matthew 27:46, KJV.

V

(1) *the astonishing actions of the saviour God. Catechism.*

(2) *the time of the daystar.* See Pseudo-Hippolytus of Rome below.

(3) *the origin of space-time remains in terra incognita.* George Smoot, cosmologist, *Wrinkles in Time,* 1993.

(4) *She [Mary] is the burning bush of the definitive theophany. Catechism.* A theophany is an appearance of God in visible form, temporary and not necessarily material. Cf. Moses and the burning bush, Exodus 3:1–15. Because Mary is theotokos, God-bearer in Greek, rendered as mother of God in English, God has appeared in her visible form temporarily, that is, during her life. Her life is therefore like the burning bush, a definitive theophany.

(5) *the time of the promises.* The promises made to Abraham concerning the promised land, Canaan, and his descendants. 'You shall be the ancestor of a multitude of nations.' Genesis 17:4, NRSV.

(6) *the remnant of Israel . . . A remnant will return, the remnant of Jacob, to the mighty God.* Isaiah 10:20–21, NRSV. The remnant of Israel survived the ravages of the nation states around it: Egypt, Assyria, Babylon.

(7) *the Suffering Servant.* Nine passages in Isaiah describe a new spirit and the character of the servant of God who will carry it out. They are the Suffering Servant and the Servant Song passages: Isaiah 11:1–2, 41:8–10, 42:1–4, 43:19, 49:1–7, 50:4–6, 52:13–15, 53:1–12, and 61:1–11. We may suppose these passages were well known to Jesus of Nazareth, because he displays a superliterate knowledge of the sacred texts. At the beginning of his ministry, at about thirty, after his baptism by John the Baptist and forty days in the wilderness, he enters the synagogue in Nazareth on the sabbath day. He is invited to read from Isaiah. He reads from the last passage in the list, 61:1–11. 'He unrolled the scroll and found the place where it was written: "The Spirit of the Lord is upon me, / because he has anointed me / to bring good news

to the poor. / He has sent me to proclaim release to the captives / and recovery of sight to the blind, / to let the oppressed go free, / to proclaim the year of the Lord's favour." And he rolled up the scroll, gave it back to the attendant, and sat down. The eyes of all in the synagogue were fixed on him. Then he began to say to them, "Today this scripture has been fulfilled in your hearing."' Luke 4:17–21, NRSV. Jesus of Nazareth said he fulfilled the scriptures of the Suffering Servant. He confirmed, and the gospels reported, the fulfilment of these scriptures, and others of significance, as the fulfilment of the Messiah, the Anointed One of God, the Christ. Jewish tradition maintains the pre-eminence of The Torah. This is The Law enshrined in The Pentateuch, the first five books of the bible.

(8) *hallowed human inhumed, unkillable in kind.* Hallowed because sanctified, human because human, inhumed because buried. Unkillable in kind because he died by the will of God: 'Not my will but yours be done.' Luke 22:42, Matthew 26:39, Mark 14:36, John 5:30, NRSV. He is dead to us just as the will of God is dead to us. We can no more kill him than we can kill the will of God. He is alive to us just as the will of God is alive to us.

(9) *Walks on the waves of a sea of light.* The risen Christ is homo-ousios with Being, the *sea of light*. This Being, ontology incarnate, is the study of the *príma philosophía* of Heraclitus (*c.* 560–*c.* 480 BC), of Parmenides (*c.* 515–*c.* 440), of Plato (*c.* 428–348 BC), and of Aristotle.

(10) *Brighter ten thousand times than the sun are the eyes of God; Christ sheds on you a light brighter than the sun.* Clement of Alexandria (*c.* 150–*c.* 215), theologian, *The Instructor; Exhortation to the Heathen. He who was 'before the daystar' and before the heavenly bodies, immortal and vast, the great Christ, shines over all being more brightly than the sun.* Pseudo-Hippolytus of Rome, after 236, 'De paschate'.

(11) *Prudence, the charioteer of the virtues.* Prudence is right reason in action. It guides the other virtues by setting rule and measure. It is the immediate guide to the judgements of conscience. *Catechism.*

(12) *Christ is the author of the life of God.* Irenaeus, 'On the Apostolic Preaching'. Cf. Acts 3:15. The risen Christ, under the protective shade of prudence, employs the heat of God, ten thousand times hotter than the sun, to forge the distinction between truth and rubbish. *In the heavens he has set a tent for the sun / . . . / and nothing is hid from its heat.* Psalm 19:4–6, NRSV.

VI

(1) *Whether we realize it or not, prayer is the encounter of God's thirst with ours. Catechism.*
(2) *Prayer is bound up with human history, for it is the relationship with God in historical events. Catechism.*
(3) *The great book . . . of history – the page on which the 'today' of God is written. Catechism.*
(4) *Contemplation is a gaze of faith. Catechism.*
(5) *the groanings of the present age. Catechism.*
(6) *Pray as if everything depended on God and work as if everything depended on you.* Attributed to Ignatius Loyola, *Catechism.*
(7) *You shall be holy, for I the Lord your God am holy.* Leviticus 19:2, NRSV.

VII

(1) *the Old Testament sets forth a philosophy of history such as the empires of the Levant never envisioned and the Greeks only later approximated . . . Judaism is a religion of history.* Roland H. Bainton, *The History of Christianity*, 1964. To think of history in this way is *to sacralise* it, to make it sacred.

(2) *the Pax Romana . . . was subject to a deep malaise. Political independence was gone . . . Men felt themselves adrift in a world grown too large, and they consequently craved such intimate fellowship as might be found in religious cults. Worse than loneliness was ennui. For many life had lost its allure . . . The mob clamoured for bread and circuses, for staged combats of beasts with beasts, of men with beasts, and of men with men . . . Nothing was done to arrest the madness . . . Freed from war, men let blood for amusement. Such avid pursuit of excitement witnesses to a profound malady of the spirit.* Bainton, op. cit. Notably, this malady of the spirit justified killing Christians by accusing them of *odium humani generis, hatred of the human race.* In this way, the *form of madness* accused its victims of its own disease. It did so *because the world is odious.* The disease takes the form of vilifying the world.

(3) *Marcion of Pontus* (died *c.* 160), was a wealthy shipowner. He believed in the god of love to the exclusion of the god of law. Because of this, he rejected the old testament and the god of law he found there. He found this god fickle, capricious, ignorant, despotic, and cruel. He was opposed by the church fathers Irenaeus, Theophilus, Tertullian, Clement of Alexandria, and Origen. Despite his belief in the god of love, Marcion despised the world. 'It is bad, said he, and *full of flies, fleas, and fevers.*' Bainton, op. cit.

VIII

(1) *Constantine.* By the first quarter of the 4th century, Constantine had emerged as emperor of the Roman empire. Christianity was *the struggle for deathlessness* because the resurrection of Christ promised the righteous immortality. 'To God, the Lord, belongs escape from death.' Psalm 68:20, NRSV. In orthodox Christian theology, the righteous conceive of death as a conception of sin. Deathlessness is a conception of sinlessness. Righteousness is equated with immortality, therefore, because Christ identified immortality and God as one and the same thing. 'And this is eternal life, that they know you, the only true God, and Jesus Christ whom you have sent.' John 17:3, NRSV.

(2) *pontifex maximus.* Constantine took this title from his pagan predecessors. He would be the bridge between man and the God of Christ. He was also the champion of *Romanitas*, that is, the inheritance of the Greek and Roman civilizations. After his victory under the banner of the cross at the battle of Milvian Bridge in 312, he was everywhere recognised by Christians as anointed by God. Under Constantine, they confessed *one God, one Lord, one faith, one baptism, one empire, and one emperor.* Bainton, op. cit. In this way, he *Linked the Romanitas of the Greco-Romans / to the holy spirit of the Byzantines.*

(3) *Tetragrammaton.* Greek, meaning four letters. The technical name for the four-letter Hebrew name of God, YHWH. Because of its sacred character, from *c.* 300 BC the Hebrews avoided uttering it when reading from scripture, substituting *Adonai*, the

Hebrew word for *Lord*, which translates to *Kyrios* in the Greek Septuagint, and *Dominus* in the Latin Vulgate. *Lord* is the word used in the NRSV and the KJV. When vowels were added to the original Hebrew text, which consisted of consonants only, the vowels in *Adonai* were inserted into YHWH. Since the 16th century, the word YaHoWaH or Jehovah was coined by this means. The original pronunciation of YHWH is thought by scholars to be Yahweh, so the word Jehovah is recent.

(4) *concordat.* Reciprocal agreement between sacred and secular authorities.

(5) *symphonia.* Harmony between sacred and secular authorities.

(6) *Theodosius.* Theodosius I, emperor from 379 to 395, established the Roman empire as a Christian state. His grandson Theodosius II, emperor from 408 to 450, embodied its law in the Theodosian Code of 438. The sentence for denying the Trinity, for example, was the death penalty. This was aimed at the followers of Arius, because they denied the full divinity of Christ. The Code also decreed that no pagans could serve in the army.

(7) Christianity became to a degree secularised. Reaction to this led to the monastic movement. The monks were *the militia christi*, the militant Christians, whose principal enemy was the Evil One. The deserts of Asia Minor, Palestine, and Egypt were their battlegrounds. Basil the Great (*c.* 330–79), one of the Cappadocian fathers, drew up the rule by which the monks lived. Benedict (*c.* 480–*c.* 550), founder of the Benedictine Order, did the same in the west *c.* 540.

IX

(1) *Justinian.* Under the emperor Justinian (*c.* 483–565), Byzantine culture acquired its definitive form, a mixture of Roman law, Christian faith, Greek philosophy, and theological speculation. The Code of Justinian in 529 sentenced Christian apostates to death by beheading. Justinian closed the schools of philosophy in Athens, also in 529.

(2) Justinian rebuilt Constantine's Church of Holy Wisdom, *Hagia Sophia*, and had it consecrated in 538. The building is, perhaps, the exemplary expression of Byzantine art.

(3) *Hagia Sophia* or *Holy Wisdom* is one of the Greek names for Christ. The Greeks had a long tradition of reverence for wisdom as a sign of the divine. The nucleus of Christianity was in the east and Greek – Byzantium, Constantinople, now Istanbul. The Greeks considered themselves custodians of the faith. Rome was to them an ecclesiastical backwater, even before Alaric the Visigoth sacked it in 410 and the Vandals pillaged it in 455.

(4) *Sacred Scripture is the speech of God as it is put down in writing under the breath of the Holy Spirit.* 'On the Word', *Vatican II.*

(5) *Man is tormented not only by pain and by the gradual breaking-up of his body but also, and even more, by the dread of forever ceasing to be.* 'Joy & Hope', *Vatican II.*

(6) *While the mind is at a loss before the mystery of death, the Church, taught by divine Revelation, declares that God has created man in view of a blessed destiny.* 'Joy & Hope', *Vatican II.*

(7) *Sacred Tradition and Sacred Scripture make up a single sacred deposit of the Word of God.* 'On the Word', *Vatican II.*

(1) *the Word of God dwelt in man, and became the Son of man, that he might accustom man to receive God, and God to dwell in man.* Irenaeus, *Refutation of All Heresies.*

(2) *St Irenaeus of Lyons repeatedly speaks of this divine pedagogy using the image of God and man becoming accustomed to one another. Catechism.* Cf. 'The eye with which I see God is exactly the same eye with which God sees me.' 'God is born in the just as the just are born in him.' Meister Eckhart (*c.* 1260–*c.* 1328), German theologian, 'Sermon 16', 'Sermon 10'.

(3) *Because man bears in himself the seed of eternity, which cannot be reduced to mere matter, he rebels against death.* 'Joy & Hope', *Vatican II.*

(4) *the all-creating furnace.* 'In what furnace was thy brain?' William Blake, 'The Tyger'.

(5) *the im- and the -possibility of the word.* Impassible means incapable of suffering, not subject to pain; incapable of feeling or emotion; incapable of change or decay. Possible means capable of suffering, subject to pain; capable of feeling or emotion; capable of change or decay. Impassible divine nature and possible human nature meet in Christ (*the word*). They are two aspects of his being.

(6) *the scriptures provide water in which lambs may walk and elephants swim.* Gregory the Great, 'Exposition of Job'.

The Teraphim of Trash

I

(1) *Cenacle.* The upper room in the house in Jerusalem where the Last Supper was celebrated. Pentecost, the baptism of the church itself by the tongues of fire of the holy spirit, also took place in the Cenacle. The Acts of the Apostles 2:1–4. 'In the Cenacle, certain signs were instituted.' '[The Eucharist] is a *signum* of that reality [of Christ's acts] and it makes a kind of anamnesis of that reality.' David Jones, 'Art and Sacrament', *Epoch and Artist*, his italics.

(2) *a hall covered with a dome, the inside of which was adorned with sapphires sparkling with a celestial blue brilliance.* A Greek traveller in the 2nd century describing a palace in Persia. This was the type on which the mosaic-encrusted interiors of Byzantine churches were modelled. *Larousse Encyclopedia of Byzantine and Medieval Art,* 1968. A Christian church was said by Epiphanius (*c.* 315–403), bishop of Salamis, to have stood on the site since the time of the emperor Hadrian (76–138). There is a group of buildings on the site today. 'The Teraphim of Trash' pictures the Cenacle as a Byzantine tribute to the original.

(3) *As a sculptor is said to have exclaimed on seeing a nude block of marble, 'What a godlike beauty you hide!', so God looks upon man in whom God's own image is hidden.* John Tauler, cited in a letter to the translator of the 1854 edition of *Theologica Germanica.*

(4) *the skeleton / Of a woman.* On 13 July 1947, this happened to George Seferis (1900–71), Greek poet: *Returning, as I was looking at the north side of the Acropolis, rocks and marble together with the Byzantine chapel below – just as one discerns faces and shapes on an old wall – I saw the tall skeleton of a woman, bones snow-white, looking at*

me with a proud air like the ghost of a hero. She looked from a world that was no longer *of today, but a future world where nothing of what I knew, things or persons, had survived. I felt the same love that I have now for life with all its beauties and evils – exactly the same love for this snow-white skeleton in the sun. A Poet's Journal, Days of 1945–1951,* his emphasis.

(5) *pallium.* The robe of a Greek philosopher. Later a special white woollen garment worn on the shoulders by the pope, a copy of which was sent to new metropolitan bishops.

(6) *colligated.* Colligate, Latin, to bind together, to connect.

II

(1) *enthusiasm.* Enthusiasmos, Greek, the entry of the god into the person.

(2) *oscillated.* She oscillates between life and death.

(3) *God called to him out of the bush, 'The place on which you are standing is holy ground.'* Exodus 3:4–5, NRSV.

III

(1) *Poets and philosophers are alike in being big with wonder.* Thomas Aquinas, 'Exposition of the Metaphysics of Aristotle.'

(2) *scop.* Anglo-Saxon for poet. Connotes to shape, form, create, like the Old Scots for poet, makar, and the Greek for maker, poeitis, from which the English word poet is derived.

(3) *fistula.* A tube of gold or silver through which the early laity received the consecrated wine of the Eucharist. Also, any natural pipe-shaped formation in a person, animal, or plant; a Roman musical pipe made from a reed.

(4) *Messinias.* Δημοσ or municipality in the southwest Peloponnese in Greece.

(5) *the Neda.* Rivers in Greece are masculine. This one, to the north of the Messinian plain, is feminine.

(6) *ecclesia domestica.* 'The Second Vatican Council, using an ancient expression, calls the family the *ecclesia domestica*.' *Catechism.*

(7) *hydromel.* A drink for good fortune and happiness. 'The Vindelici [in the southern Baltic] worship Fortune, and putting her idol in the most eminent situation, they place a horn in her right hand, filled with that beverage made of honey and water, which by a Greek term we call *hydromel.* St Jerome proves, in his eighteenth book on Isaiah, that the Egyptians and almost all the eastern nations do the same.' William of Malmesbury (*c.* 1090–*c.* 1143), English historian, *The Kings Before the Norman Conquest.*

(8) *chiparo.* A translucent Greek spirit made from grape skins.

(9) *lekythos.* A white urn placed next to a body in a grave, often with a white-winged Nike or Victory painted on it. 5th century BC Attic pottery, mature period 470–460 BC.

IV

(1) *The birdman of the minimalist.* The *Mayflies* are symbols of creatures coming into being one moment and leaving it another. Because they have *DNA* and *wings*, each is *the birdman of the minimalist*, because its small size and short life express the topos of *the birdman* in minimal form. This topos or motif, found throughout the world, reaches into prehistory. Examples of it are common. Angels, archangels, cherubim, seraphim, sphinxes and other creatures (man or animal) depicted with wings, the Zu-bird of Akkadian legend who stole the Tablets of Destiny, the human figure with the bird in the cave at Lascaux, Christ as an eagle leading souls to heaven – painted on a stone column in the Basilica of Saint Julien in Brioude in France: all have one thing in common. Wings as symbols of spiritual flight. 'Those who know have wings.' *Pancavimsa Brahmana*, cited by Mircea Eliade, *Shamanism: Archaic Techniques of Ecstasy*, 1964. Spiritual intelligence is symbolised by 'the image of the soul in the form of a bird.' Eliade, op. cit.

(2) *Junkyard palaces.* Hectares of beds, boxes, fridges, tables, sinks, coffins, and anything else, piled in the open on top of one another, to be sold to discerning customers.

(3) *The teraphim of trash.* The household gods or icons of junk culture.

(4) *The athlete of Christ.* John Cassian (*c.* 360–*c.* 430), monk, *Institutes of the Coenobia*.

(5) *Alpheos.* The Alpheos flows through the largest river valley in the Peloponnese. Olympia, from where we get the Olympic Games, is on its banks.

(6) *that Pythagorian maxim: 'Follow God'.* Boethius, *The Consolation of Philosophy.* Seneca (*c.* 4 BC-65 AD), Roman moralist, *mentions that there was an old proverb when anyone was exhorted to endure adversity, 'Follow God'.* John Calvin (1509–64), French theologian, *The Institutes of the Christian Religion.*

V

(1) *Naked yourself follow a naked Christ.* Jerome, letter to Rusticus of Narbonne.

(2) *I am become like a leather bottle in the frost.* Jerome, letter to Eustochium. He is 39, she is 15. He is quoting Psalm 118:83 in the Latin Vulgate.

(3) *Be the cicada of the night.* Jerome, letter to Eustochium. He is echoing Virgil (70–19 BC), 'Eclogue II'.

(4) *gongles.* A neologism. The verb imitates the sound made by the brass bells worn round the necks of sheep and goats to communicate with their shepherd.

(5) *the village.* The village of Sitochorion in the vicinity of Trifilias in the municipality of Messinias. Mount Ithome, known to Homer, *c.* 9th century BC, as the 'step-mountain', because of its sharp rise from the plain, is visible from the village.

(6) *the seven gifts of the holy spirit.* These are wisdom, understanding, counsel, strength, knowledge, piety, terror of God. Cf. Isaiah 11:1–3.

VI

(1) 'There is in her [*Sapientia* or Sophia or Wisdom] a spirit that is intelligent, holy / . . . / For she is a breath of the power of God, and a pure emanation of

the glory of the Almighty; / therefore nothing defiled gains entrance into her. / For she is a reflection of eternal light, / a spotless mirror [speculum sine macula] of the working of God / . . . / in every generation she passes into holy souls / and makes them friends of God . . . / She is more beautiful than the sun, / and excels every constellation of the stars.' The Wisdom of Solomon, 7:23–29, NRSV. *[The holy spirit] is called the wisdom of God.* Irenaeus, 'On the Apostolic Preaching'.

(2) *The fear of the Lord is the beginning of wisdom.* Psalm 110:10, KJV.

(3) *This is the distance [to] the new Golden Age . . . And the centuries that intervene are a foul, agnostic welter through the Stygian seas of mud: a long* Scavenger Age, *inevitable where the Mother of Abominations has long dwelt.* Thomas Carlyle (1795–1881), Scottish writer, 'Latter-Day Pamphlet', his emphasis.

(4) *Now like the spawn of fish they float in the ocean.* Sumerian poet, 3rd millennium BC, 'The Story of the Flood', *The Epic of Gilgamesh*, translated by N. K. Sandars.

(5) *The cursèd lust for gold.* Virgil, *The Aeneid* 3:56–7.

(6) *Lightning flashed from Mount Sinai, / And I beheld it; / Let me bring you at least a spark.* Háfiz (c. 1326–c. 1390), Persian poet, Sufi philosopher, 'Ghazal 455', *In Search of Háfiz*, translated by A. J. Alston. Bounded on the north by the mountains of Arcadia, and on the south and west by the Ionian Sea, Messinias was invaded from the east by the Spartans. In the 4th century BC, the Messinians built a stone city, surrounded by a stone wall seven kilometres long, to defend themselves. The ancient city of Messene on *Mount Ithome* is an active archaeological site, funded by the European Union, on a par with Delphi and Olympia.

(7) *The makar's wierd is to be a wanderer.* Anglo-Saxon poet, c. 7th century?, 'Widsith', translated by Michael Alexander. Wierd or weird means fate or destiny.

(8) *Wanderer, rider of the storm.* The poet's destiny is to be a wanderer, riding the storm of life, to wonder.

(9) *Why are the sacred stones destroyed?* 'The Search for Everlasting Life', *The Epic of Gilgamesh*. The destruction of the sacred stones is linked in some way, which is unexplained, with the failure of Gilgamesh in his quest for immortality.

(10) *There is one Sumerian fragment which says that a righteous soul shall not die.* N. K. Sandars, introduction, *The Epic of Gilgamesh. the good / shall never die.* Sumerian poet, 2500–1800 BC, 'The Sumerian Underworld'. *Poems of Heaven & Hell from Ancient Mesopotamia*, Sumerian fragment, translated by N. K. Sandars. 'Righteousness is immortal.' The Wisdom of Solomon 1:15, NRSV. 'For to know you [God] is complete righteousness, / and to know your power is the root of immortality.' The Wisdom of Solomon 15:3, NRSV. 'The righteous live by their faith.' Habakkuk 2:4, NRSV, late 7th to early 6th century BC. Cited in The Letter of Paul to the Romans 1:17; The Letter of Paul to the Galatians 3:11; and The Letter to the Hebrews 10:38. 'Grappling with the interpretation of this verse led Martin Luther to question the prevailing doctrine of justification [by indulgences and the treasury of merits], ultimately precipitating the Protestant Reformation.' David W. Baker, *New Bible Commentary: 21st Century Edition*. 'The righteous shall have a blessed end.' Surah 28, 'The Story', *The Koran*.

VII

(1) *the queen's lyre.* The model was a reconstruction in the British Museum of a lyre found in royal graves, Sumerian city of Ur, *c.* 2500 BC. Inlaid with mother-of-pearl, it has a sound-box ending in a gold bull's head.

(2) *obsidian dagger.* Obsidian, or *volcanic glass*, was one of the most precious substances in antiquity, in hardness second only to diamond. The island of *Milos* in Greece: a rich source.

(3) *Can a burnt-out lamp / Catch light from the candle of the sun?* Háfiz, 'Ghazal 2', *In Search of Háfiz.*

(4) *Come, Sufi, for the cup is a clear mirror / In which to behold the purity of the ruby wine.* Háfiz, 'Ghazal 7', *In Search of Háfiz.* Gilgamesh meets Siduri, 'the woman of the vine, the maker of wine'. Sufi poets like Rumi (1207–73) and Háfiz used the figure of the wine-bearer as a guide to reality. Siduri directs Gilgamesh to Urshanabi, who ferries him over the waters of death, where he meets Utnapishtim. 'To him alone of men the gods had given everlasting life.' *The Epic of Gilgamesh.* Utnapishtim offers Gilgamesh the immortality of the gods, if he keeps vigil for a week. Gilgamesh fails this last test in his quest. 'A mist of sleep like soft wool teased from the fleece' came over him.

VIII

(1) *Háfiz is drunk on the wine of eternity / And no one will find him sober again.* Háfiz, 'Ghazal 45', *In Search of Háfiz.* The wine of eternity is identified in the Sufi tradition with good tidings, good news, gospels. 'Drunk and desolate in a corner of the tavern, / I heard last night – how can I describe it? – / Good tidings through an angel from Beyond.' Háfiz, 'Ghazal 37', *In Search of Háfiz.* The angel Gabriel, who dictated *The Koran* to Muhammad.

(2) *Protagoras quipped that man is the measure of all things.* Aristotle, *The Metaphysics.*

(3) *behold I am dying for want of wise meaning, and insight into the devouring fact: speak, if you have any wisdom!* Thomas Carlyle, 'Life of Sterling'.

(4) *No person is insulted when almighty God is given precedence over him.* Ambrose, letter to the Christian emperor Valentinian, who was eight or nine at the time.

(5) *Justicia immortalis est.* Justice is immortal. Alternative translation of The Wisdom of Solomon 1:15.

IX

(1) *The lyrebird of futurity.* The lyrebird, like the peacock, is a symbol of immortality, that is, of God. The bird of the queen's lyre is the spiritual intelligence of Sapientia, who takes her form here from the vision of George Seferis. She is from the future not the present or the past.

(2) *There is the house whose people sit in darkness; dust is their food and clay their meat. They are clothed like birds with wings for covering, they see no light, they sit in darkness. I entered the house of dust and I saw the kings of the earth, their crowns put away for ever; rulers and princes, all those who once wore kingly crowns and ruled the world in the days of old.* The underworld or Sheol in *The Epic of Gilgamesh. Such as sit in darkness and in the*

shadow of death. Psalm 107:10, KJV. *The dayspring from on high hath visited us, to give light to them that sit in darkness and in the shadow of death.* The Gospel According to Luke 1:79, KJV.

(3) *rets.* Soaks, softens, seasons, rots.

(4) *Rain is considered as great a manifestation of the divine power as the resurrection of the dead.* Philip Birnbaum, *Encyclopedia of Jewish Concepts*, 1993.

X

(1) *the auricles of his heart.* The *auricles* and *ventricles* of Christ's heart.

(2) *bdellium.* A substance mentioned in Genesis 2:12 variously taken to be a gum resin from India, Persia, and Africa; a precious stone; a kind of amber. It is here a symbol of Christ's blood as it *pours on the floor* of Sheol *molten* and *on fire* to reach the damned.

(3) *What would it pleasure me, to have my throat cut / With diamonds? or to be smothered / With cassia? or to be shot to death, with pearls?* John Webster (*c.* 1580–*c.* 1625), English poet and playwright, *The Duchess of Malfi* 4:2.

(4) *tempora christi.* Latin, the time of Christ. The Christian dispensation.

(5) *it is easy to miss Him / at the turn of a civilization.* David Jones, 'A, a, a, Domine Deus'.

(6) *Bede.* The Venerable Bede (*c.* 673–735), the candle of the church, father of English history, doctor of the church, foremost scholar in Anglo-Saxon England, prototypical English monk. Author of *Ecclesiastical History of the English People* and other works. He follows in the footsteps of the church fathers Augustine, Jerome, Ambrose, and Gregory the Great. He lived in the time of the illuminated *Lindisfarne Gospels* and the Anglo-Saxon epic poem *Beowulf.*

(7) *Language is the house of the living . . . / the poet its signature.* 'In *Hölderlin und das Wesen der Dichtung* (1936) [Heidegger] treats of language as the house of Being and of the poet as the guardian of Being.' *The Oxford Dictionary of the Christian Church*, 1997. Martin Heidegger (1889–1976), ontological philosopher.

(8) *My conductor drew me strongly after him; and in this manner we ascended lofty fiery mountains, from which arose lakes, and burning rivers, and all kinds of metal seething, wherein I found immersed innumerable souls.* 'The Vision of Charles the Fat', crowned Carolingian emperor of the west, 25 December 880. Cited by William of Malmesbury, *The Kings Before the Norman Conquest.*

(9) *the abysmal depths of personality.* Augustine, *The City of God.*

The Argosy of Faith

I

(1) *I lie in the tomb of my sins, bound in the chains of iniquity . . . in chains to Babylon, that is, to the babel of a distracted mind.* Jerome, letter to Chromatius, Jovinus, and Eusebius.

(2) *my belly wishes to be my god in Christ's place: lust urges me to drive away the holy spirit.* Jerome, letter to Heliodorus.

(3) *argosy.* A merchant ship of large size and tonnage.

(4) *the voyaging of the Christian soul . . . the argosy of the Son of God . . . the argosy of Christ.* David Jones, 'An Introduction to the Ancient Mariner', *The Dying Gaul*.

(5) *Believe love when it tells you the truth.* Jerome, letter to Chromatius, Jovinus, and Eusebius.

(6) *How then can a mortal be righteous before God? / . . . / the stars are not pure in his sight.* Job 25:5, NRSV.

(7) *Love inclines and unites the human spirit to God.* Gilbert of Hoyland (d. 1172), Cistercian monk, 'Sermon 11 on the Song of Songs'.

(8) *The word of God was given her . . . by an open infilling of her reason.* Guibert of Gembloux, Walloon monk, *Life of Hildegard of Bingen*. Last secretary to Hildegard. She was a visionary musician and medic (1098–1179).

II

(1) *I will be the pattern of all patience.* William Shakespeare, Lear, *King Lear* 3:2.

(2) *horrible steep. extreme verge. delicate stratagem.* Gloucester [who has been blinded]: *Methinks the ground is even.* Edgar: *Horrible steep.* Edgar: *Give me your hand; you are now within a foot / Of the extreme verge.* Lear: *It were a delicate stratagem to shoe / A troop of horse with felt.* William Shakespeare, *King Lear* 4:6.

(3) *Christians are made, not born.* Latin, Christiani fiunt, non nascuntur. Tertullian (c. 160–c. 225), African church father, father of Latin theology.

(4) *You have been surfeited to nausea as though with the flesh of quails.* Jerome, letter to Furia, a young, rich, noblewoman living in Rome. He is echoing Numbers 11:31.

(5) *The Greeks have a pretty proverb: 'A fat paunch never breeds fine thoughts.'* Jerome, letter to Nepotian.

(6) *the abiding penalties of the ancient malediction.* William of St Thierry (c. 1075–1148), theologian, 'Meditation 6'.

(7) *the cradlings of a new-born faith.* Jerome, letter to Heliodorus.

(8) *Give me a lover's humility.* Ignatius Loyola, 'Spiritual Diary'.

(9) *I have passed beyond the limits of consolation, and in forbidding you to weep for one man's death I have mourned for the dead of the whole world.* Jerome, letter to Heliodorus.

III

(1) *My heart is numbed, my hand trembles, my eyes are misty, my tongue stammers . . . I can think of nothing but his death . . . What shall we do, O my soul? Whither shall we turn? . . . Where now is that comely face, where is that dignified figure? O grief! the lily withered when the south wind blew, and the violet's purple slowly faded into paleness.* Jerome, letter to Heliodorus.

(2) *the world was oppressed with diverse extreme and sore calamities long before the Redemption.* Augustine, *The City of God*.

(3) *like so much dust thrown up off the face of the earth I am turned into the plaything of the winds.* William of St Thierry, 'Meditation 9'. *like chaff that the wind drives away.* Psalm 1:4, NRSV.

(4) *Before thy coming [O Saviour Christ] was there anything more miserable than man, who cowering in eternal fear of death had but received the sense of life that he might perish?* Jerome, letter to Heliodorus.

IV

(1) *Parchments are dyed purple, gold is melted for lettering, manuscripts are decked with jewels.* Jerome, letter to Eustochium.

(2) *Our walls glitter with gold, gold gleams upon our ceilings and upon the capitals of our pillars: yet Christ is dying at our doors in the persons of his poor, naked and hungry.* Jerome, letter to Pacatula.

(3) *men whose courage was as conspicuous in their sorrows as in their wars.* Jerome, letter to Heliodorus.

(4) *Words fail; for language is inadequate to the greatness of this theme.* Jerome, letter to Heliodorus.

V

(1) *Make creels of reeds or weave baskets of pliant osiers. Hoe the ground and mark it out into equal plots, and when you have sown cabbage seed or set out plants in rows, bring water down in channels . . . Graft barren trees with buds or slips . . . Make hives for bees.* Jerome, letter to Rusticus.

(2) *I have learned by experience that the ass on the high road makes for an inn when it is weary.* Jerome, letter to Laeta.

(3) *a language capable of expressing a religious apprehension of reality.* Jeremy Hooker, *New Welsh Review*, Winter 1989/1990.

(4) *O power of the divine power, O strange energy! / . . . / How in your essence totally divine do you mingle yourself with grass?* Symeon the New Theologian (949–1022), Byzantine theologian and poet.

(5) *Blessed Jesus, with what fervour and zeal did she [Fabiola] study the sacred volumes!* Jerome, letter to Oceanus on the death of Fabiola.

(6) *the uncreated light.* Symeon described visionary light as *uncreated* and eternal, the light of God. This is identified in the Greek hesychast way of prayer with the light which shone from Christ on Mount Tabor during the Transfiguration. Cf. Matthew 17:1–13, Mark 9:2–13, Luke 9:28–36. Hesychast, Greek hesychia, inner stillness, quietness, silence of the heart. The tradition of prayer associated with the monks of Mount Athos.

(7) 'We should follow him up the mountain of our naked intelligence, even as Peter, James, and John followed him up *Mount Tabor.*' John of Ruysbroeck (1293–1381), mystical writer, 'The Sparkling Stone'.

VI

(1) *the mighty souls that dwell within . . . feeble bodies.* Jerome, letter to Laeta.

(2) *Death then died when Life died on the tree.* Latin, Mors mortua tunc est, in ligno quando mortua vita fuit. Written on the cross in the baptistry of St Peter's in Rome, 6th century. *Daily Missal.*

(3) *Have a set of letters made for her [Paula], of boxwood or of ivory.* Jerome, letter to Laeta.

(4) *the magic spring time of the sacred story.* John McManners, *Oxford Illustrated History of Christianity*, 1996.

(5) *Paul, you are mad; your great learning is turning you mad.* The Acts of the Apostles 26:24, R[evised] S[tandard] V[ersion].

(6) *a God-shaped emptiness.* John Crowley (b. 1941), bishop of Middlesbrough, at the Funeral Mass of Cardinal Basil Hume, Westminster Cathedral, 25 June 1999.

(7) *How comes sure knowing of things, and especially knowledge about God? Is it through reasoned proof, or through a faith which acts; and which is the earlier, the faith that acts, or proof by reasoning?* Anthony of Egypt (c. 251–356), father of Christian monasticism, to two Greek philosophers, who had come to see him. They answer that the faith that acts comes earlier, and that this is the sure knowledge. Anthony: '*You say well, for that faith comes from the very build of the soul, but the art of logic from the skill of those who framed it.*' Athanasius (c. 296–373), bishop of Alexandria, *St Anthony of the Desert*, 1995, translated by Dom J. B. McLaughlin.

(8) *In every rank and condition of life, the very bad is mingled with the very good.* Jerome, letter to Rusticus.

VII

(1) *I will not venture beyond the grasp of my intelligence.* Hilary of Poitiers (c. 315–c. 368), bishop of Poitiers, 'On the Trinity'.

(2) *There is a saying of Plato that a wise man's whole life should be a preparation for death.* Jerome, letter to Heliodorus. Cf. Plato, *Phaedo.*

(3) *I follow the prophetic way.* 'Who among the poets has not drunk from the fountain of the prophets?' Tertullian, *Apology.* 'What is Plato, but Moses speaking in Attic Greek?' Numenius, 2nd century, Pythagorean philosopher, cited by Clement of Alexandria, *The Stromata.*

(4) *We part with arrogance less easily than with gold and jewels.* Jerome, letter to Oceanus.

(5) *Swarms of Huns had poured down from the distant Sea of Asov, midway between the icy river Tannis and the savage tribes of the Massagetae, where the gates of Alexander [the Caspian Gates] keep back the barbarians behind the rocky Caucasus . . . Children were forced to die, who had only just begun to live, and in ignorance of their fate smiled amid the brandished weapons of their foe.* Jerome, letter to Oceanus.

VIII

(1) *The army standards bear the emblem of the cross . . . The Armenians have laid aside their quivers, the Huns are learning the psalter, the frosts of Scythia are warmed by the fire of faith. The ruddy, flaxen-haired Getae carry tent-churches about with their armies.* Jerome, letter to Laeta.

(2) *a familiar garden.* The Garden of Eden.

IX

(1) *Christ . . . of prophets the sole Archprophet of the Father.* Eusebius of Caesarea, *The History of the Church.*

(2) *Epiclesis.* Invocation of the holy spirit.

(3) *Moloch, horrid king besmeared with blood / Of human sacrifice.* John Milton, *Paradise Lost*, bk. 1, 392.

(4) *odium theologicum.* Theological hatred. 'Is not this a fearful judgement of God and a cruel wrath that the very prelates and shepherds of our souls, which were wont to

feed Christ's flock with Christ's doctrine are now so sore changed that if they smell that one of their flock do but once long or desire for the true knowledge of Christ, they will slay him, burning him with fire most cruelly.' William Tyndale (1494–1536), translator of the bible, *The Obedience of a Christian Man*. His remark is historically accurate. A law called *De Haeretico Comburendo* was passed in 1401, in the reign of Henry IV, aimed at the Lollards. They were followers of John Wycliffe (*c.* 1330–84), theologian and philosopher. They translated the bible into English *c.* 1380–92. Under the new law, reading or owning or sharing such a bible in English was punishable by fines, imprisonment, and burning at the stake. *Statutes of the Realm* 2:125. Tyndale's translation of the bible into English, which forms the greater or the essential part of the KJV, has helped to shape the western mind. In 1535 he was arrested, imprisoned at Vilvorde near Brussels, strangled and burnt at the stake, probably on 6 October 1536. 'Bigotry is the disease of the religious.' Heraclitus, *Herakleitos & Diogenes*, op. cit.

(5) *alethiology*. Greek, alíthea, truth, the not hidden. The study of truth.

(6) *alembicated*. An alembic is a gourd-shaped vessel used in distilling. It has a long beak or neck which conveys the products to a receiver. *The hot spirit drawn out of the alembic of hell*, Edmund Burke (1729–97), political philosopher. Moloch's eyes are *alembicated* in the sense that they are on the end of long, extendable stalks, which retract or *suck back to hell*; and *alembicated* in the sense of being on the end of the optic nerve of the alembic of hell . The stalks are prehensile but *stiff-necked* in the sense of obstinate, stubborn, inflexible.

(7) *Between a rock and a hard place*. Between the devil and the deep blue sea. Between hell and high water.

(8) *shtum*. Yiddish, quiet, silent.

(9) *schola cantorum*. The school of singers trained in church services established by Gregory the Great. The Roman chant was brought to Britain by Benedict Biscop (*c.* 628–*c.* 689), mentor of Bede, and Wilfrid (634–709), bishop of York. The cathedral choir school, as in Canterbury Cathedral, is a descendant of this.

(10) *matris fons*. Latin, mother, plus spring, fountainhead, source. As in the town Motherwell in Scotland.

(11) *osculatorium*. A plate of ivory, wood, or metal with a crucifix on its surface, with a handle for conveying the Kiss of Peace. Latin, osculum, a kiss. The plate was kissed then passed on to someone else to kiss. The practice is now obsolete. The Kiss of Peace became the Sign of Peace made by shaking hands during Mass. The Kiss or Sign of Peace is Apostolic. 'Greet one another with a holy kiss.' The Letter of Paul to the Romans 16:16. 'Greet one another with a kiss of love.' The First Letter of Peter 5:14, NRSV.

(12) *illapse*. Gentle sinking in.

(13) *Those who laugh with Satan will never be able to rejoice with Christ*. Peter Chrysologos (*c.* 400–450), bishop of Ravenna. Cited in *Daily Missal*.

X

(1) *filius iniquitatis*. The son of iniquity, Satan, the devil, the Evil One. Renunciation of the devil is an early attested rite in baptism. Hippolytus (*c.* 170–*c.*

236), *The Apostolic Tradition*. The son of iniquity is derived from Ezekiel 28:11–19. Ezekiel to the king of Tyre, 'you were on the holy mountain of God; / you walked among the stones of fire. / You were blameless in your ways / from the day that you were created, / until *iniquity* was found in you.' NRSV. There are similar verses in Isaiah directed at the king of Babylon, known as 'the light-bearer'. 'How art thou fallen from heaven, O Lucifer, son of morning! . . . For thou hast said in thine heart, I will ascend to heaven, I will exalt my throne above the stars of God.' Isaiah 14:12–13, KJV. When Jesus says to his followers, 'I saw Satan fall like lightning from heaven', Luke 10:18, RSV, *the son of iniquity, Lucifer, and Satan* coalesce to form one identity to personify evil. Paul made it clear evil did not originate, as in the first two cases, in political corruption alone. 'Put on the whole armour of God, so that you may be able to stand against the wiles of the devil. For our struggle is not against enemies of flesh and blood, but against the rulers, against the authorities, against the cosmic powers of this present darkness, against the spiritual forces of evil in the heavenly places.' The Letter of Paul to the Ephesians 6:11–12, NRSV.

(2) *lux eterna*. English, eternal light, a title of Christ, *Daily Missal*.

(3) *tower of strength*. Latin, turris fortitudinis, a title of Christ, *Daily Missal*.

(4) *ivory tower*. Latin, turris eburnea, a title of Mary, *Daily Missal*.

(5) *desire of eternal hills*. Latin, desiderium collium eternorum, a title of Christ, *Daily Missal*.

(6) *and after the fire a still small voice*. 1 Kings 19:12, KJV. *Sometimes I hear the voice of your [God's] spirit, a passing whisper like the faintest breeze*. William of St Thierry, 'Meditation 2'.

(7) *Paráclitos*. Greek for advocate. The Paraclete, the spirit of truth. John 14:16–17, 16:7.

(8) *you can turn me into an intelligible utterance of God*. Ignatius of Antioch (*c*. 35–*c*. 107), 'Epistle to the Romans', before his martyrdom in the Colosseum.

(9) *Our soul is escaped as a bird out of the snare of the fowlers*. Psalm 124:7, KJV. *No one will snatch them out of my hand*. John 10:28, NRSV.

(10) *Like the morning star among the clouds / . . . / like the sun shining on the temple of the Most High / . . . / like a cypress towering in the clouds*. Sirach 50:6–10, NRSV.

Against the Deadening of the Mind

I

(1) *Rock-graven epigram, madrigal of fact*. Absolute certainty of fact. Singing about it.

(2) *hubristic*. Insolent, contemptuous. Hubris, Greek hybris, presumption, especially about God; sets its own tragedy in motion.

(3) *Nobody is so blind or so stupid as to believe that they can reach perfect understanding; indeed, the deeper their understanding, the more they are conscious of their ignorance*. Basil the Great, 'On Faith'.

(4) *He who has seen the whole world hanging on a hair of the mercy of God has seen the truth . . . the cold truth*. G. K. Chesterton, *Saint Francis of Assisi*, 1923.

(5) *deadening of the mind.* John of the Cross (1542–91), Spanish poet, *Dark Night of the Soul.*

(6) *He who is without love . . . should be diagnosed as spiritually dead.* Thomas Aquinas, 'On the Perfection of the Spiritual Life'.

(7) *paten.* The dish for bread in the Eucharist.

(8) *plate.* Ecclesiastical utensils made of metal.

(9) *corrody.* Provision for maintenance. Ecclesiastical tenure or pension.

(10) *to coin anything worth notice out of the mintage of antiquity.* William of Malmesbury, *The Kings Before the Norman Conquest.*

(11) *carts.* 'Between 1050 and 1350 in France alone several million tons of stone were quarried and carted to construct 80 cathedrals, 500 large churches, and thousands of smaller church buildings . . . During the construction of Chartres Cathedral, the inhabitants of the town harnessed themselves to *carts*, nobles, children, everybody, to *haul the stones; they tugged in silence.*' Roland H. Bainton, op. cit.

(12) *O God of Truth / Keep him who tells this story straight.* Patrick Kavanagh (1904–67), poet, 'Lough Derg'.

II

(1) *Rome, thy departed glory moan, / And weep thy luminaries gone.* Cited by William of Malmesbury, *The Kings Before the Norman Conquest.* From the epitaph of Henry III (d. 1056), emperor of the Germans.

(2) *locking the stable door after the horse has bolted*: In the face of the truth about it, it was no use the church adopting a policy of silence and denial. *flogging a dead horse.* It was no use compounding sin with more sin. The way out, as theology teaches, was orthodox contrition, confession, and supplication for forgiveness. On the first Sunday of Lent, 12 March 2000, Pope John Paul II apologised to God from the altar of St Peter's Basilica in Rome for 2000 years of sin committed by the church. His apology confessed seven sins. (1) Sin in general. (2) Sins against the Jews. (3) Sins of fanaticism and zealotry in the service of the faith, such as the Crusades against the Muslims and the Inquisition. (4) Sins of schism, persecution, and wars of religion, vitiating Christian unity. (5) Sins against women. (6) Sins against different cultures, different ways of being. (7) Sins against fundamental human rights. If concrete details flesh out these abstractions, the result is a revelation of evil. By confessing to it, the church is in possession of it. That is to say, in practical terms, in possession of the documentation of the evils it has itself committed. These lead, by extension, to the evils committed in the world outside the church. The sacred deposit of the church is therefore a deposit of both good and evil.

(3) *Those literary characters who are kept in obscurity either by the malevolence of fame, or the slenderness of their fortune.* William of Malmesbury, *The Kings Before the Norman Conquest.*

(4) *Marranos.* Spanish, origin obscure. A term of opprobrium for conversos, Jews or Muslims converted forcibly or otherwise to Christianity. The word *marrano* came to mean filthy, pig, pork, persona grosera, filthy swine. Since pork is forbidden to Jews, the insult was pointed.

(5) *Sanbenitos.* Penitential garments ordered by the Inquisition to be worn for a

period or for life. Short sleeveless yellow cloaks with red St Andrew's crosses on the back and front. The people who wear these.

(6) *anamnesis.* Remembrance, the not forgetting of things past. 'The Holy Spirit . . . awakens the memory of the Church.' *Catechism.*

(7) *irenics.* Greek. The theology of peace. Irene and Rene are names derived from it, meaning peace.

(8) *Samarra.* A black or grey sanbenito with the likeness of the person, resting on burning torches surrounded by demons, painted or embroidered on it.

(9) *relaxing.* To relax was the official term for the condemnation of persons by the church to the secular authorities for burning at the stake. 'They were normally given the choice between repenting before the auto de fe reached its climax, in which case they were "mercifully" strangled when the flames were lit; or remaining unrepentant, in which case they were roasted alive.' Henry Kamen, *The Spanish Inquisition,* 1965/1998.

(10) *after Mass.* Joseph del Olmo, *Relación Histórica del Auto General de Fe que se celebró en Madrid este año de 1680,* Madrid, 1680, contemporary source of the following account published in London in 1748: 'When they had finished the Celebration of the Mass the King withdrew and the Criminals who had been condemn'd to be burnt were delivered over to the Secular Arm, and being mounted upon Asses were carried through the Gate called Foncaral, and at Midnight near this Place were all executed.' Kamen tells us: 'The procedure at this auto represented the fully developed practice of the Inquisition.' 'There was no age limit for those condemned to the stake: women in their eighties and boys in their teens were treated in the same way.' 'The death rate was . . . heavily weighted against people of Jewish and Muslim origin.' 'The terrible reality [was] that most of the mortal victims of the Spanish Inquisition were of Jewish origin.' *The Spanish Inquisition.*

III

(1) *Pornocracy.* 'In the tenth century, . . . the papacy had become again the preserve of Italian families . . . two domineering women of ill repute, Theodora and Marozia, . . . dictated papal appointments . . . this era in papal history has been called the *Pornocracy.*' Bainton, op. cit.

(2) *The catechetical tradition recalls that there are 'sins that cry to heaven'. Catechism.*

(3) *To labour is to pray.* Latin, laborare est orare. *The Rule of St Benedict.*

(4) *the triple concupiscence that subjugates [man] to the pleasures of the senses, covetousness for earthly goods, and self-assertion, contrary to the dictates of reason. Catechism.* Concupiscence means vehement desire.

(5) *shooting up.* Injecting drugs with a hypodermic syringe.

(6) *episcopus.* A bishop. Greek, epi, over, scopos, inspector. Overseer.

(7) *the history of sin.* In Christian theology, death is the consequence of sin. So this also reads *the history of death.*

IV

(1) *poetpops.* Poetasters. *OED*: A paltry poet; a writer of trashy verse.

(2) *His head was as bald as the polished surface of a cocoa-nut shell.* Herman Melville (1819–91), novelist and travel writer, *Typee; or the Marquesas Islands*, 1847.

(3) *History repeats itself, first as tragedy, and then again as tragedy.* Louis de Bernières, *Captain Correlli's Mandolin.*

(4) *palanquin.* A covered litter for one person carried by two or more men by poles projecting before and after.

(5) *consubstantial.* Co-equal, of one substance, homo-ousios.

V

(1) *the River Lee unlost.* Of the many tributaries of the River Thames, most of them are lost to view, covered over and channelled underground in iron tubes, concrete tunnels. The River Lee is not covered over.

(2) *He is the image of the invisible God.* The Letter of Paul to the Colossians 1:15. *The Holy One of Israel is Christ, who became visible to men.* Irenaeus, 'On the Apostolic Preaching'. *Christ . . . the natural image of the invisible God.* Bonaventura, *The Mind's Road to God.*

(3) *A man's worth is what he is in the sight of God, and no more.* Francis of Assisi, cited by Bonaventura, *The Life of Saint Francis.*

(4) *the lean and strenuous personality of Jesus.* H. G. Wells (1866–1946), writer, *The Outline of History,* 1920.

(5) *that strange cry of ecstasy, never heard before, sent a thrill of wonder through the Christian world.* Maxwell Staniforth, editor, on the ecstasy of martyrdom described by Ignatius of Antioch, 'The Epistle to the Romans', *Early Christian Writings,* 1968.

VI

(1) *No man blessed / with a happy land-life is like to guess / how I, aching-hearted, on ice-cold seas / have wasted whole winters.* Anglo-Saxon poet, *c.* 7th century?, 'The Seafarer', translated by Michael Alexander.

(2) *Why hast thou set me as a mark against thee, so that I am a burden to myself?* Job 7:20, KJV.

(3) *Wherefore, since God . . . is the master and guide of this blind soul, it may well and truly rejoice, once it has learned to understand this, and say: In darkness and secure.* John of the Cross, *Dark Night of the Soul.*

(4) *these obscure and afflictive dark waters of God.* John of the Cross, *Dark Night of the Soul.*

(5) *When God finished speaking with Moses on Mount Sinai, he gave him the two tablets of the covenant, tablets of stone, written with the finger of God.* Exodus 31:18. *Have pity on me, O you my friends, / for the hand of God has touched me!* Job 19:21. *If it is by the finger of God that I cast out demons, then the kingdom of God has come to you.* Luke 11:20, NRSV.

(6) *Elohim.* 'Elohim or God is the preferred term for God as the Creator of the universe; and for God as the God of foreigners. Yahweh or the Lord is the

preferred term for the covenant partner of Israel.' Gordon J. Wenham, *New Bible Commentary*.

VII

(1) *turn, return, repent* all translate the Hebrew term teshuvah, 'denoting a return to God after sin, as opposed to meshuvah, which means backturning, apostasy. Maimonides devotes ten chapters to teshuvah.' Philip Birnbaum, *Encyclopedia of Jewish Concepts*.

(2) *The Lord once called you [the Hebrews], A green olive tree, fair with goodly fruit.* Jeremiah 11:16, NRSV. 'If the root is holy, then the branches also are holy. But if some of the branches were broken off, and you, a wild olive shoot, were grafted in their place to share the rich root of the olive tree, do not boast over the branches. If you do boast, remember that it is not you that support the root, but the root that supports you.' The Letter of Paul to the Romans 11:16–18, NRSV. '[The church] draws nourishment from that good olive tree [Judaism] onto which the wild olive branches of the Gentiles have been grafted.' 'Our Age', *Vatican II*.

(3) *Jerusalem. You who would remind the Lord, / take no rest, / and give him no rest / until he establishes Jerusalem.* Isaiah 62:6–7, NRSV. *I will be a wall of fire all around [Jerusalem], says the Lord, and I will be the glory within it.* Zechariah 2:5, NRSV.

(4) *a divine vocation is always pure and clear.* Ignatius Loyola, *Spiritual Exercises*.

(5) *the tender-hearted and seraphic Assisian [Francis of Assisi].* Francis Thompson, *Saint Ignatius Loyola*.

(6) *The eyes of the soul must be cleansed before God can be seen.* Theophilus of Antioch (115–181), bishop of Antioch, 'Theophilus to Autolycus'. *tears whereby the inner eye is cleansed, that it may avail to see God.* Bonaventura, *Life of St Francis*.

(7) *like the full moon at the festal season; / . . . / like lilies by a spring of water, / . . . / like a vessel of hammered gold / studded with all kinds of precious stones.* Sirach 50:6–9, NRSV.

VIII

(1) 'Be courteous when you argue with *the People of the Book*.' Surah 29, 'The Spider', *The Koran*.

(2) *a trinity of man.* Jews, Christians, Muslims.

(3) *No common God mistook.* 'Where wast thou when I laid the foundations of the earth?' 'Canst thou bind the sweet influences of Pleiades, or loose the bands of Orion?' Job 38:4, 31, KJV.

(4) *The whole of creation is small to the soul that sees the Creator.* Gregory the Great, 'Life of Benedict'. *He brings the Creation into being and will then restore it.* Surah 10, 'Jonah', *The Koran*. *I was well aware that the universe is great and huge, beautiful and good, but the reason why it seemed so small was that I saw it in the presence of him who is its Creator.* Julian of Norwich, *Revelations of Divine Love*.

(5) *It is a world wet with the blood of people slaughtering each other.* Cyprian (d. 258), bishop of Carthage, 'To Donatus'.

(6) *I was like a gentle lamb / led to the slaughter.* Jeremiah 11:19, NRSV. *The Word of God was led in silence to the slaughter.* Cyprian of Carthage, 'On the Benefit of Patience'.

IX

(1) *Whoever God has enriched nobody shall impoverish.* Cyprian of Carthage, 'To Donatus'.

(2) *Whoever is kind to the poor lends to the Lord.* Proverbs 19:17, NRSV. *It is not anything of yours that you are bestowing on the poor; rather, you are giving back something of [God's].* Ambrose, 'On Naboth'.

(3) *Gold and silver are tried in the fire.* Cited by Cyprian of Carthage, 'On the Death Rate'.

(4) *I cry you mercy, Lord.* Margery Kempe, *The Book of Margery Kempe*.

(5) *I have tested you in the furnace of adversity.* Isaiah 48:10, NRSV.

(6) *genii.* Plural of genius, a genie, a jinnee, a jinn. The winged intelligence officers of the spirit.

(7) *The Lord knows those who are his.* The Second Letter of Paul to Timothy 2:19, NRSV.

X

(1) *Neither honey nor spice gives wine the taste that a real thirst gives to water.* Ailred (1109–67), abbot of Rievaulx, *On Spiritual Friendship*.

(2) *God, who, as he is immortal himself, had put a coal, a beam of immortality into us, which we might have blown into a flame, but blew it out by our first sin.* John Donne (1571–1631), poet and Dean of St Paul's, *Devotions Upon Emergent Occasions*, 1624.

(3) *Rob not God, nor the Poor, lest thou ruin thyself; the Eagle snatcht a Coal from the Altar, but it fired her Nest.* Benjamin Franklin (1706–90), *The Sayings of Poor Richard*.

(4) *What more valuable than Gold? Diamond. Than Diamonds? Virtue.* Benjamin Franklin, op. cit.

(5) *I have thrown myself into the hands of Almighty God.* Patrick, mid to late 5th century, apostle of the Irish, *The Confession*. *Only they who fly home to God have flown at all.* Patrick Kavanagh, 'Beyond the Headlines'.